The Lost Gospels

The Lost Gospels

Mark M. Mattison

Also by Mark M. Mattison

The Gospel of Mary:
A Fresh Translation and Holistic Approach

The Gospel of Judas:
The Sarcastic Gospel

The Gospel of Thomas:
A New Translation for Spiritual Seekers

The Gospel of Q:
Jesus' Prophetic Wisdom

The Gospel of Philip:
The Divine Mysteries of Marriage and Rebirth

The Gospel of Peter:
Revisiting Jesus' Death and Resurrection

The Gospel of Truth:
The Mystical Gospel

The Infancy Gospels:
Exploring Jesus' Family

The Secret Book of James:
How to be Whole

The Nativity of Mary
as Revealed by James

The Odes of Solomon:
Jesus' Songbook

First Edition

Luminescence, L.L.C., Publisher
www.luminescence-llc.net
Grand Rapids, Michigan

Cover art: Armenian manuscript binding of Walters Art Museum Ms. W.538

Dedicated
to the Loving Memory of
our son, Gabriel

CONTENTS

יְהֹוָה
SIMEON
LEVI
IVDAH
DAN
GAD
ASHER
ISACAR
IOSEPH
PETER
ANDRE
IAMES
IOHN
PHILIP
THOM
IAMES
SIMON
IVDE
Cum Priuilegio.

Preface

What are "the Lost Gospels"? Where do they come from, and why weren't they included in the Bible?

The most popular collection of extrabiblical Jewish and Christian books is Rutherford H. Platt, Jr.'s *The Lost Books of the Bible,* first published in 1926. The title is misleading, however, since most of the texts in Platt's collection were never truly "lost," nor were they ever included in the Bible to begin with. By contrast, most of the Gospels in this collection were literally "lost"—in most cases, written in the second century, copied and recopied for a few hundred years, then lost to history for over a thousand years before one or more manuscripts were discovered in the nineteenth or twentieth century. Here's a partial chronology:

1886-1887	The Gospel of Peter discovered near Achmim
1896	The first known manuscript of the Gospel of Mary purchased from an antiquities dealer in Cairo
1897	The first Greek fragments of the Gospel of Thomas discovered at Oxyrhynchus
1945	A library containing Egyptian translations of the Gospel of Truth, the Gospel of Thomas, the Gospel of Philip, and the Secret Book of James discovered near Nag Hammadi
1970s	The Book of the Stranger and the Gospel of Judas discovered near El Minya

I began translating these Gospels from Greek and Egyptian in 2013, after I became interested in the practice of Christian mysticism. I found some of these Gospels, particularly the Gospels of Thomas and Mary, to be deeply spiritual and personally meaningful.

This immediately raises the question of whether these Gospels should have been, or should be, included in the New Testament. That's really a question about the "canon" or "rule" of the Bible—specifically, which books are included and which books aren't. It's not really a straightforward question, because it's inseparable from questions about institutional authority in the church. Traditionally, many Christians have defined Christianity in terms of three **C**s: **c**reed, **c**anon, and **c**lergy, with each mutually reinforcing the other. Organized churches generally seek consistency between their beliefs (creed), their authoritative texts (canon), and their designated authorities (clergy). Canonical texts (as defined by the clergy) are consistent with the church's creed; the church's creed in turn is based on its canon; and its clergy, authorized by its canons, maintain the accuracy of its creed. In other words, the authority of the three **C**s is self-referential (which is why I define Christian churches by means of a different three **C**s: "**C**hrist-**c**entered **c**ommunities," irrespective of the other three **C**s).

So, to ask about changes to the "canon" of scripture is really to ask what changes different church institutions are inclined to make. Different institutional churches already have different canons (along with different creeds and different criteria for clergy). The Catholic canon is larger than the Protestant canon, and the Orthodox canon is larger than the Catholic canon. What one church considers "apocrypha," another considers part of their Bible. Canons of Scripture, then, are defined by the institutions that use them. Enlarging or restricting their canons, in other words, is entirely up to them.

That said, there's undoubtedly immense benefit to studying early Gospels that weren't ultimately included in the traditional church institutions' New Testament canon. I do consider them Scriptural texts, and find some of them to be at least as inspiring and thoughtful as the New Testament's four Gospels. Other people will have different reactions and experiences entirely, which is as it should be. People are different, and our needs aren't always the same. Not everyone is at the same point in their spiritual journey.

How can these two ideas be held in tension—i.e., that other Gospels can be read as Scripture without necessarily being part of the New Testament's canon? Here it's helpful to consider the difference between *Scripture* and *canon*. They overlap, clearly, because Biblical canons preserve faith communities' definitive sacred Scriptures. But Scriptures (i.e., sacred writings) don't need to be canonical to be read and appreciated. As the idea of a canon slowly emerged in the early church, Jesus' followers understood this well.

For example, an early document known as the Muratorian fragment discusses which books should be included in the Christian canon. When it comes to a popular second-century book named the Shepherd of Hermas, the Muratorian fragment states that it "ought to be read," but goes on to state that "it cannot be made public in the church to the people, nor placed among the prophets, as their number is complete, nor among the apostles to the end of time." So, the author didn't think the Shepherd of Hermas should be publicly read in church, although it was still valuable and "ought to be read" privately. It wasn't to be included in the liturgy, but that didn't mean it was to be shunned.

On the other hand, the Muratorian fragment goes on to argue that some books should be "rejected" entirely, including the writings of Valentinus. This reflects the fact that early followers of Jesus debated which texts to use. But what the Muratorian fragment also shows is that the canon was fluid in the first few centuries, and that it can be helpful to study extracanonical books. To that end, hopefully this current collection will prove valuable to students of Christian history and spirituality. Not necessarily to redefine or replace a particular canon of Scripture, but to enhance our understanding about the development of early Christianity and to deepen our appreciation of multiple perspectives.

It may also be helpful to consider the availability of these translations. One of the reasons I set out to translate these texts in the first place is because with few exceptions (like the Gospel of Peter and the Infancy Gospels), public domain versions of these Gospels were simply not available. Not only did I want to write about and quote these Gospels; I wanted to enable others to do exactly the same thing. Consequently, I prepared public domain translations and first published them on my Academia site (https://independent.academia.edu/MarkMattison), then on https://www.gospels.net, a website which was generously given to me by Andrew Bernhard. These public domain versions have been duplicated on several sites and in several apps and books, which is exactly what I wanted to see since I believe some version of these books should belong to the world, not just one person or business. However, in addition to posting public domain versions, I've also published my own titles with different translations of these same Gospels. As in my other books, the versions in this book differ somewhat from my public domain translations. Another difference is that the current volume doesn't include notes on proposed reconstructions, textual variants, and alternative readings; for those additional details, please refer to my other titles.

Readers who have followed my work over the years may note nuanced adjustments in my translation strategies. Some of the changes in this volume are intended to create more consistency across translations. One of the more noteworthy differences is that although I've still worked to minimize masculine generic language (including, but not limited to, the popular use of the singular "they"), I haven't consistently removed gendered divine pronouns, since some texts (particularly the Egyptian ones) intentionally use both masculine and feminine divine pronouns. Yet other changes are merely stylistic.

This work involves more than translation principles, however. In recent years, I've grown increasingly interested not only in the art of translation, but in its visual presentation as well. To date, I've published three books featuring full photographs of the original manuscripts as artistic illustrations. My goal has been to deepen readers' appreciation of the texts with a multimedia experience.

Also in recent years, friends have encouraged me to publish a one-volume collection of my Gospel translations, but I wasn't sure how to go about formatting and organizing such a volume. Then I reflected on the fact that Platt's popular anthology, *The Lost Books of the Bible,* followed the format of the King James Version of the Bible, including justified double columns, drop caps, chapter headings, and chapter summaries. Consequently, it occurred to me to see what these texts might look like in a similar format, based on the format and design of the original 1611 King James Version and its faithful copycat, Platt's early twentieth-century collection of ancient Jewish and Christian books that weren't included in the Bible. And, like Platt's volume, I'd include black-and-white illustrations; specifically, sixteenth century woodcuts.

There are a number of other questions. The most pressing is how to divide the texts into chapters and verses. Some texts, like the Gospel of Thomas, the Gospel of Peter, and the Infancy Gospel of James, have already been assigned chapter and verse numbers by earlier generations of scholars. However, many other recovered Gospels don't have any such agreed-upon chapter and verse divisions. Usually, scholars cite these manuscripts only by page and line numbers. In the end, where there was already a numbering system in place, I used it. Where there wasn't, I didn't make up my own verse numbers, because that could make it more difficult to compare my translations to the translations of others. With respect to most of the Gospels written in Egyptian, although I've introduced chapter breaks, I've retained the page numbers of the original manuscripts in bold print for ease of reference.

Editorial elements such as chapters, verses, summaries, arrangement of text, etc., form the "paratext" of the Gospels—that is, a framework of interpretation that may or may not reflect the perspective of the original author. Frameworks of interpretation are actually inherent in every iteration of a text. For example, it's sometimes possible to discern different potential meanings between a second-century Greek version of a text and a fourth-century Egyptian translation of the same text by considering their different contexts. The same can be said of contemporary Bibles, which typically provide outlines, headings, cross-references, and annotations to assist readers in navigating through the Biblical text consistent with a particular interpretation (for example, a Catholic or an evangelical Protestant interpretation).

Mindful of these dynamics, I've usually tried to reflect elements in the text itself when preparing the interpretative framework. Summaries of chapters, for example, tend to reflect the language used in the text itself. Occasionally, however, I've taken the opportunity to provide some clarifying commentary in the chapter summaries.

Readers will encounter various editorial symbols throughout these translations. For convenience, those symbols are listed on the next page:

Editorial Symbols

[...] Gap in the text

[ ] Hypothetical reconstruction of missing text due to gaps in the manuscript

( ) Editorial insertion to clarify the text

< > Proposed editorial correction of a scribal error

<...> Unintelligible word or phrase

1 Bold numerals indicate page numbers of original papyri

Sayings
Gospels
SIMEON
LEVI.
IVDAH
DAN.
GAD
ISACAR
ZABVL
IOSEPH
IAMES
IOHN
PHILIP
THOM
IAMES
SIMON
IVDE
Cum Priuilegio.

THE GOSPEL OF Q

he text of "Q" (*Quelle,* or "source") is a hypothetical reconstruction of a Greek source used by the Gospels of Matthew and Luke. It's based on the widespread thesis that Matthew and Luke independently copied much of Mark's Gospel; if neither Matthew nor Luke knew of each other's Gospels, one must account for the approximately 200 verses with nearly word-for-word agreement between Matthew and Luke but not found in Mark. The hypothesis (first proposed by Christian Hermann Weisse in 1838) is that in addition to Mark's narrative Gospel, they both copied an otherwise lost "sayings source." For more information, see my book, *The Gospel of Q: Jesus' Prophetic Wisdom,* published in 2016.

As a hypothetical reconstruction, Q appears to have been written in Galilee in the first century, reflecting many early teachings of Jesus, depicted as a prophet of Wisdom anointed as the Son of God.

CHAP. I.

John exhorts the crowds to repent. The axe lies at the root of the trees. John baptizes in water, but one who's greater will baptize in Holy Spirit and fire.

ohn [...] the entire region around the Jordan [...]

He said to the crowds who went out to be baptized, You offspring of vipers, who warned you to flee from the fury to come? So bear fruit worthy of repentance! Don't start to say to yourselves, We have Abraham for our ancestor, because I tell you that God is able to raise up children for Abraham from these stones.

Even now the axe lies at the root of the trees! So every tree that doesn't bear good fruit is cut down and thrown into the fire.

I baptize you in water, but one who's greater than I will

come, the thong of whose sandals I'm not worthy to loosen. He'll baptize you in Holy Spirit and fire. His pitchfork is in his hand to clean out his threshing floor, and to gather the wheat into his barn; but he'll burn up the chaff with a fire that can't be put out.

CHAP. II.

Jesus is baptized and then tempted by the devil.

esus [...] baptized [...] heaven opened and [...] the Spirit [...] on him [...] Son [...]

Jesus was led by the Spirit into the desert to be tested by the devil. He didn't eat anything for forty days [...] he was hungry.

And the devil said to him, If you're God's Son, tell these stones to turn into bread.

And Jesus replied, It's written, A person shouldn't live on bread alone.

The devil led him to Jerusalem, set him on the pinnacle of the temple, and said, If you're God's Son, throw yourself down, because it's written, God will put his angels in charge of you, and on their hands they'll bear you up, so that you don't dash your foot against a stone.

And in response Jesus said to him, It's been said, Don't test the Lord, your God.

Then the devil took him to a very high mountain and showed him all the empires of the world and their glory and said to him, I'll give you all these, if you'll bow to me.

And in response Jesus said to him, It's written: Bow to the Lord your God, and serve God only.

And the devil left him.

CHAP. III.

The beatitudes. Love your enemies. Treat people how you want them to treat you. Don't judge. Get the beam out of your own eye. No good tree bears rotten fruit. The parable of the house on the sand.

azareth [...] He looked up at his disciples and said:

Blessed are you who are poor, because yours is God's kingdom.

Blessed are you who are hungry, because you'll be full.

Blessed are you who mourn, because you'll be comforted.

Blessed are you when they criticize you, persecute you, and spread lies about you because of the Son of Humanity.

Rejoice and be glad, because your heavenly reward is great; for that's how they persecuted the prophets before you.

Love your enemies, and pray for those who persecute you. You'll become children of your Father, who makes the sun rise on those who are evil and those who are good, and sends rain on those who are just and those who are unjust.

When someone slaps you on the cheek, offer the other one too. When someone sues you for your shirt, give them your coat too. When someone makes you go one mile, go an extra mile. Give to everyone who asks you, and when someone borrows your things, don't ask for them back.

Treat people how you want them to treat you. If you love those who love you, why should you be rewarded? Don't even toll collectors do that? And if you lend to those from whom you expect repayment, why should you be rewarded? Don't even gentiles do that? Be merciful, just like your Father.

Don't judge, and you won't be judged; because you'll be judged the way that you judge. And you'll be measured the way that you measure.

Can someone who doesn't see guide another person who doesn't see? Won't they both fall into a pit? A disciple isn't greater than their teacher. It's enough for the disciple to become like their teacher.

Why do you see the speck that's in your brother's (or sister's) eye, but don't consider the beam that's in your own eye? How can you tell your brother (or sister), Let me get that speck out of your eye, when you don't see the beam that's in your own eye? You hypocrite! First get the beam out of your own eye, and then you'll see clearly to get the speck out of your brother's (or sister's) eye.

No good tree bears rotten fruit, nor does a rotten tree bear good fruit. Every tree is known by its own fruit. Are figs gathered from thorns, or grapes from thistles? The person who's good brings good things out of their good treasure, and the person who's evil brings evil things out of evil treasure, because one's mouth speaks from the overflow of the heart.

Why do you call me, Master, Master, and don't do what I say? Everyone who hears my words and acts on them can be compared to someone building a house on bedrock.

When the rain poured, and the floods came, and the winds blew and pounded that house, it didn't collapse, because it was founded on bedrock. But everyone who hears my words and doesn't act on them is like someone who built a house on the sand. When the rain poured, and the floods came, and the winds blew and pounded that house, it collapsed immediately. How great was its fall!

CHAP. IV.

Jesus heals a centurion's boy. Jesus is amazed at the centurion's faith.

nd so when it happened that he had finished saying these things, he went to Capernaum. A centurion approached and begged him and said, My boy is sick.

And Jesus said to him, I'll go heal him.

And the centurion replied, Master, I'm not worthy for you to come under my roof. Just say the word, and my boy will be healed. I'm also in a chain of command, with soldiers under me. I tell one, Go, and they go; I tell another, Come, and they come; I tell my servant, Do this, and they do it.

Jesus was amazed when he heard this. He said to his followers, I'm telling you, I haven't found such faith even in Israel.

CHAP. V.

John sends his disciples to ask Jesus whether he is the coming one. Jesus talks to the crowd about John. Wisdom is vindicated by her children.

hen John heard all these things, he sent his disciples to ask him, Are you the coming one, or should we look for someone else?

And he replied to them, Go and tell John what you've heard and seen. Those who:

don't see, regain their sight;
have challenges of mobility, walk;
have leprosy, are cured;
don't hear, hear;
are dead, are raised up;
are poor, have good news announced to them.

Blessed is the one who isn't scandalized by me.

And when they had left, he started to talk to the crowds about John: What did you go out into the desert to see? A reed shaken by the wind? Then what did you go out to see? A man wearing fancy clothes? Look, those who wear fancy clothes live in palaces. Then what did you go out to see? A prophet? Yes, I'm telling you, and much more than a prophet, because it's written about him:

> Look, I'm sending my messenger ahead of you, who'll prepare your path for you.

I'm telling you that John is greater than anyone who's been born, but whoever is least in God's kingdom is still greater than he, because John came to you [...] the toll collectors and [...] but [...] him.

To what, then, can I compare this generation? What's it like? It's like children sitting in the marketplaces calling to each other, We played the flute for you, but you didn't dance. We mourned, but you didn't weep.

John didn't come eating or drinking, and you say, He's demonized! The Son of Humanity has come eating and drinking, and you say, Look, a glutton and a drunk, a friend of toll collectors and outsiders!

But Wisdom is vindicated by her children.

CHAP. VI.

Following Jesus. The harvest is plentiful. Galilean towns do not respond to Jesus' deeds.

nd someone said to him, I'll follow you wherever you go.

And Jesus said to him, Foxes have holes and birds of the sky have nests, but the Son of Humanity has nowhere to rest his head.

But someone else said to him, Master, let me go and bury my father first.

But he said to him, Follow me, and let the dead bury their own dead.

He said to his disciples, The harvest is plentiful, but the workers are few. So ask the Lord of the harvest to send workers into the fields. Go! Look, I send you out like lambs among wolves. Don't carry a purse, bag, sandals, or staff. Don't greet anyone on the road. Whenever you enter a house, first say, Peace to this house. If a peaceful person is there, let your blessing rest on them; but if not, take back your blessing. Stay in the same house, eating and drinking whatever they give you, because the worker is worthy of their wages. Don't move around from house to house. If they welcome you in whatever town you enter, eat whatever is set before you. Heal those who are sick there and tell them, God's kingdom is at hand! But if they don't welcome you in whatever town you enter, when you're leaving that town, shake the dust from your feet. I'm telling you that on that day, it'll be better for Sodom than for that town!

Woe to you, Chorazin! Woe to you, Bethsaida! If the great deeds done in your midst had been done in Tyre and Sidon, they would have repented a long time ago in sackcloth and ashes. But it will be better for Tyre and Sidon than for you in the judgment! And you, Capernaum, you don't think you'll be exalted to heaven, do you? You'll fall down to Hades!

Whoever welcomes you welcomes me, and whoever welcomes me welcomes the one who sent me.

CHAP. VII.

Jesus prays to the Father and teaches how to pray. Ask and you'll receive.

Then he said, Thank you, Father, Lord of heaven and earth, for hiding these things from the wise and learned and revealing them to children. Yes, Father, this was what you wanted. My Father has given me everything. No one knows who the Son is except the Father, or who the Father is except the Son, and the one to whom the Son wants to reveal him.

Blessed are the eyes that see what you see. I'm telling you that many prophets and rulers wanted to see what you see, but didn't see it; and to hear what you hear, but didn't hear it.

When you pray, say: Father, we honor your holy name. Let your kingdom come. Give us our daily bread today. Forgive us our debts, because we too forgive everyone who's indebted to us. Don't put us in harm's way.

I'm telling you, ask and you'll receive. Look and you'll find. Knock and it'll be opened for you, because everyone who asks receives. The one who looks finds. To one who knocks it'll be opened. Which of you would give your child a stone if they ask for bread? Or who would give them a snake if they ask for fish? So if you, evil as you are, know how to give good gifts to your children, how much more will the heavenly Father give good things to those who ask!

CHAP. VIII.

Overcoming Demonic Power. A divided house will fall. Whoever isn't with Jesus is against him.

e was casting out a demon that couldn't speak. And when the demon came out, the person who couldn't speak started talking. And the crowds were amazed. But some said, He casts out demons with the power of Beelzebul, the ruler of the demons!

Knowing what they were thinking, he said to them, Every divided empire is devastated, and a divided house will fall. If the Enemy is divided, how will its empire endure? But if Beelzebul gives me power to cast out demons, who gives your people power to cast them out? So they prove you wrong. But if I cast out demons by the finger of God, then God's kingdom has come to you!

Whoever isn't with me is against me, and whoever doesn't gather with me, scatters. When the impure spirit leaves someone, it journeys through arid places looking for rest, but doesn't find it. Then it says, I'll return to the home I left; and when it comes back, it finds it swept and organized. Then it goes out and brings seven other spirits that are even more evil, and they move in and live there. That person ends up even worse off than before.

CHAP. IX.

Some demand that Jesus show a sign. No one lights a lamp and hides it. Jesus pronounces woes upon Pharisees and lawyers. Nothing is concealed that won't be revealed. Don't be afraid of those who kill the body but can't kill the soul.

ome demanded that he show a sign. But he said, This is an evil generation. It demands a sign, but no sign will be provided except the sign of Jonah! As Jonah became a sign to the Ninevites, so the Son of Humanity will be a sign to this generation. The queen of the South will rise up in the judgment with this generation and will condemn it, because she came from the ends of the earth to hear Solomon's wisdom; and look, something greater than Solomon is here. The people of Nineveh will rise up in the judgment with this generation and will condemn it, because they repented in response to Jonah's announcement, and look, something greater than Jonah is here.

No one lights a lamp and hides it, but puts it on a lampstand, and it enlightens everyone in the house. Your eye is the body's lamp. If your eye is single, your whole body is full of light. If your eye is evil, your whole body is dark. So if the light within you is dark, how dark it is!

Woe to you, Pharisees! You tithe your mint, dill, and cumin, but you ignore justice, mercy, and faith. You should've done these without ignoring the others.

Woe to you, Pharisees! You clean the outside of the cup and dish, but inside they're full of greed and decadence. Clean the inside of the cup, and its outside will be clean too.

Woe to you, Pharisees! You love the place of honor at banquets, the front seat in the synagogues, and accolades in the marketplaces. Woe to you, because you're like unmarked graves that people walk on without knowing it.

And woe to you, lawyers! You load people with burdens that are hard to bear, but you yourselves won't even lift a finger to help them.

Woe to you, lawyers! You shut people out of God's kingdom. You didn't enter, and didn't let those enter who are trying to do so.

Woe to you, because you build the tombs of the prophets whom your ancestors killed. You prove that you're the descendants of your ancestors. So Wisdom said, I'll send prophets and sages. Some of them they'll kill and persecute.

So this generation will be guilty of the blood of all the prophets shed from the beginning of the world, from the blood of Abel to the blood of Zechariah, who died between the altar and the sanctuary. Yes, I'm telling you that this generation will be held responsible.

Nothing is concealed that won't be revealed, nor hidden that won't be made known. Whatever I tell you in the dark, say in the light; and whatever you hear whispered in your ear, announce from the housetops.

Don't be afraid of those who kill the body but can't kill the soul. Instead, fear the one who can kill both the soul and the body in Gehenna.

CHAP. X.

More valuable than sparrows. Acknowledging the Son of Humanity. Don't store treasures here on earth, but in heaven. Don't worry. The parable of the faithful and wise servant. Jesus came to cast fire on the earth. Interpreting the time. Settle with your adversary.

on't five sparrows cost two pennies? Yet not one of them will fall to the ground without your Father's permission. Even the hairs of your head are all numbered. Don't be afraid, because you're more valuable than many sparrows.

Everyone who publicly acknowledges me, the Son of Humanity will acknowledge in front of the angels. But whoever publicly denies me will be denied in front of the angels. Whoever speaks out against the Son of Humanity will be forgiven, but whoever speaks out against the holy Spirit won't be forgiven. When they bring you before the synagogues, don't worry about how or what you should say, because the Holy Spirit will teach you at that time what you should say.

Don't store treasures for yourselves here on earth, where moth and rust destroy and robbers break in and steal. Instead, store treasures for yourselves in heaven, where neither moth nor rust destroy and where robbers don't break in or steal. Because where your treasure is, there your heart will be too.

So I'm telling you not to worry about your life, about what you'll eat; or about your body, what you'll wear. Isn't life more than food, and the body more than clothes? Think about how the ravens don't sow, reap, or gather into barns, yet God feeds them. Aren't you more valuable than the birds?

Which of you can grow any taller by worrying? And why worry about clothes? Look at how the lilies grow. They don't work or spin, yet I'm telling you that even Solomon in all his glory wasn't dressed like one of these. But if God clothes the grass of the field, which is here today and is thrown into the oven tomorrow, won't he clothe you even more, you who have little faith? So don't worry. Don't ask, What are we going to eat? or, What are going to drink?

Albrecht Altdorfer, The Last Judgment, ca. 1513
Metropolitan Museum of Art

or, What are we going to wear? The gentiles look for all these things, but your Father knows that you need all of them. Instead, look for God's kingdom, and all these things will be given to you too.

But know this: If the master of the house had known at what time the robber was coming, he wouldn't have let his house be broken into. You too should be ready, because the Son of Humanity is coming when you don't expect it.

Then who is the faithful and wise servant who was entrusted by their master to hand out rations to the household at the right time? Blessed is that servant whose master finds them doing so when he comes. I'm telling you the truth: he'll put them in charge of all that he owns. But if that servant says in their heart, My master is late, and starts to beat the other servants and to eat and drink with those who are addicted to alcohol, the master of that servant will come when they don't expect it, at a time that they don't know, and will rip them to shreds and throw them out with those who are faithless.

I came to cast fire on the earth, and how I wish it were already kindled! Do you think that I came to bring peace on earth? I didn't come to bring peace, but a sword! Because I've come to pit son against father, daughter against her mother, daughter-in-law against her mother-in-law.

He said to them, When it's evening, you say, There'll be good weather, because the sky is red. In the morning, There'll be wintry weather today, because the sky is red and threatening. You know how to interpret the appearance of the sky. Why don't you know how to interpret the time?

When you're going with your adversary, do your best to settle the case on the way there, or else your adversary may hand you over to the judge, and the judge to the officer, and the officer may throw you into prison. I'm telling you that you won't get out of there until you've paid the very last penny!

CHAP. XI.

The parables of God's kingdom. Enter through the narrow door. Many from east and west. Jerusalem kills the prophets. Whoever exalts themselves will be humbled, and whoever humbles themselves will be exalted. The parable of the great dinner. Whoever tries to find their life will lose it. Salt is good. No one can follow two masters. The Law and the Prophets were announced until John. Everyone who divorces his wife and remarries is unfaithful. The parables of the lost sheep and the lost coin. Forgiveness and faith.

hat is God's kingdom like, and to what should I compare it? It can be compared to a mustard seed which someone sowed in their garden. It grew and became a tree, and the birds of the sky nested in its branches.

And again: To what should I compare God's kingdom? It can be compared to yeast which a woman hid in fifty pounds of flour until it was all fermented.

Enter through the narrow door, because many will try to enter, though only a few will succeed. When the master of the house gets up and locks the door, you'll be standing outside and knocking on it, saying, Master, open up for us! But he'll reply, I don't know you. Then you'll start saying, We ate and drank with you, and you taught in our streets. But he'll tell you, I don't know you. Get away from me, you criminals!

Many will come from east and west and dine with Abraham, Isaac, and Jacob in God's kingdom, but you'll be thrown out into the outer darkness, where there'll be weeping and grinding of teeth. Those who are last will be first, and those who are first will be last.

Jerusalem, Jerusalem, who kills the prophets and stones those who are sent to her! How often I would've gathered your children together, like a hen gathers her chicks under her wings, but you wouldn't let me! Look, your house is left abandoned. I'm telling you that you won't see me until the time comes when you say, Blessed is the one who comes in the name of the Lord!

Whoever exalts themselves will be humbled, and whoever humbles themselves will be exalted.

Someone planning a great dinner invited many guests. When dinner was ready, they sent their servant to tell the invited guests, Come, because it's ready now!

One excused himself because of his farm. Another excused himself because of his business. The servant went back and told their master all this. Then the master of the house became angry and told the servant, Go out to the highways and urge people to come in so that my house may be filled.

Whoever doesn't hate father and mother can't be my disciple, and whoever doesn't hate son and daughter can't be my disciple. Whoever doesn't carry their own cross and follow me can't be my disciple.

Whoever tries to find their life will lose it, but whoever loses their life for my sake will find it.

Salt is good, but if it's lost its flavor, how can you get it back? It's no good for the soil or the manure pile. It's thrown away.

No one can follow two masters, because they'll either hate one and love the other, or they'll be devoted to one and despise the other. You can't serve both God and money.

The Law and the Prophets were announced until John. Since then, God's kingdom has been violated, and the violent plunder it. But it's easier for heaven and earth to disappear than for one smallest letter or one tiny pen stroke to drop out of the Law.

Everyone who divorces his wife and remarries is unfaithful to her, and whoever marries someone who's divorced is unfaithful too.

There's no way that people won't be tripped up, but woe to the one who causes it! It'd be better for them if a millstone were hung around their neck and they were thrown into the sea, than for them to trip up one of these little ones.

Which of you, if you had a hundred sheep and lost one of them, wouldn't leave the ninety-nine in the hills and go after the one that got lost? When they find it, I'm telling you that they'll rejoice over it more than over the ninety-nine that didn't wander off.

Or what woman with ten silver coins, if she loses one, wouldn't light a lamp, sweep the house, and look everywhere until she found it? When she finds it, she calls together her friends and neighbors and says, Rejoice with me, because I've found the coin that I'd lost! In the same way, I'm telling you, the angels rejoice over one sinner who repents.

If your brother (or sister) offends you, correct them. If they repent, forgive them. Even if they offend you seven times a day, then forgive them seven times.

If you had faith as big as a mustard seed, you could tell this mulberry tree, Be uprooted and be planted in the sea, and it would obey you.

CHAP. XII.

The coming of God's kingdom can't be observed. As it was in the days of Noah, so it will be in the day of the Son of Humanity. The parable of the minas. Sitting on thrones.

hen he was asked when God's kingdom would come, he replied to them, The coming of God's kingdom can't be observed. Nor will they say, Look over here! or, Look over there! Because, look, God's kingdom is among you.

If they tell you, Look, he's in the desert! don't go out; or Look, he's inside! don't follow, because as the lightning flashes in the east and is seen in the west, so will the Son of Humanity be in his day. Where there's a corpse, there the vultures will gather.

As it was in the days of Noah, so it will be in the day of the Son of Humanity. In those days they were eating and drinking, marrying and giving in marriage, until the day that Noah entered the ark, and the flood came and swept all of them away. That's what it will be like on the day the Son of Humanity is revealed.

I'm telling you, there'll be two men in the field; one will be taken and the other will be left. There'll be two women grinding at the mill; one will be taken and the other will be left.

A certain person went on a trip. He called ten of his servants, gave them ten minas, and said to them, Do business with this until I return.

After a long time the master of those servants returned to settle accounts with them. The first one came and said, Master, your mina has made ten more minas.

He said to him, Well done, good servant! Since you've been faithful with a little, I'll put you in charge of much.

The second came and said, Master, Your mina has made five minas.

He said to him, Well done, good servant! Since you've been faithful with a little, I'll put you in charge of much.

The other came and said, Master, I know you're a strict man, reaping where you didn't sow and gathering where you didn't scatter. I went out and hid your mina in the ground. Look, here's what belongs to you!

He said to him, You evil servant! You knew that I reap what I didn't sow and gather where I didn't scatter? So why didn't you invest my money with the bankers? Then when I returned, I would've gotten it back, with interest. So take the mina away from him and give it to the one who has ten minas, because everyone who has will be given more, but whoever doesn't have will lose even what little they do have.

You who've followed me will sit on thrones, judging the twelve tribes of Israel.

THE GOSPEL OF THOMAS

he Gospel of Thomas currently survives in three third-century Greek fragments (discovered in the late nineteenth and early twentieth centuries) and one complete fourth-century Egyptian translation (discovered in a library of books unearthed in 1945). It was originally written in Greek in the first or second century. For more information, see my book, *The Gospel of Thomas: A New Translation for Spiritual Seekers,* published in 2015.

This Gospel is noteworthy as a collection of sayings rather than a traditional narrative Gospel. As such, it closely resembles (and often overlaps) the hypothetical reconstructed text of Q. As an esoteric text, this Gospel is opaque at times, inviting readers to ponder its meanings. Spiritual unification (making "the two into one") is a principal feature of this book.

Scholars have divided the book into 114 discrete sayings or *logia.* That numbering system has been retained in this translation.

PROL.

hese are the hidden sayings that the living Jesus spoke and Didymos Judas Thomas wrote down.

SAYING I.

Discovering meaning.

nd he said, Whoever discovers the meaning of these sayings won't taste death.

SAYING II.

Seeking and finding.

esus said, Whoever seeks shouldn't stop until they find. When they find, they'll be disturbed. When they're disturbed, they'll be [...] amazed, and reign over everything.

SAYING III.

Seek the kingdom within.

esus said, If your leaders tell you, Look, the kingdom is in heaven, then the birds of heaven will precede you. If they tell you, It's in the sea, then the fish will precede you. Rather, the kingdom is within you and outside of you.

When you know yourselves, then you'll be known, and you'll realize that you're the children of the living Father. But if you don't know yourselves, then you live in poverty, and you are the poverty.

SAYING IV.

Many who are first will be last.

esus said, The older person won't hesitate to ask a little seven-day-old child about the place of life, and they'll live, because many who are first will be last, and they'll become one.

SAYING V.

What's hidden will be revealed.

esus said, Know what's in front of your face, and what's hidden from you will be revealed to you, because there's nothing hidden that won't be revealed.

SAYING VI.

Jesus' disciples ask questions about public ritual.

is disciples asked him, Do you want us to fast? And how should we pray? Should we make donations? And what food should we avoid?

Jesus said, Don't lie, and don't do what you hate, because everything is revealed in the sight of heaven; for there's nothing hidden that won't be revealed, and nothing covered up that will stay secret.

SAYING VII.

The lion and the human.

esus said, Blessed is the lion that's eaten by a human and then becomes human, but woe to the human who's eaten by a lion, and the lion becomes human.

SAYING VIII.

The parable of the fisher.

e said, The human being is like a wise fisher who cast a net into the sea and drew it up from the sea full of little fish. Among them the wise fisher found a fine large fish and cast all the little fish back down into the sea, easily choosing the large fish. Anyone who has ears to hear should hear!

SAYING IX.

The parable of the sower.

esus said, Look, a sower went out, took a handful of seeds, and scattered them. Some fell on the roadside; the birds came and gathered them. Others fell on the rock; they didn't take root in the soil and ears of grain didn't rise toward heaven. Yet others fell on thorns; they choked the seeds and worms ate them. Finally, others fell on good soil; it produced fruit up toward heaven, some sixty times as much and some a hundred and twenty.

SAYING X.

Jesus casts fire on the world.

esus said, I've cast fire on the world, and look, I'm watching over it until it blazes.

SAYING XI.

Those who are living won't die.

esus said, This heaven will disappear, and the one above it will disappear too. Those who are dead aren't alive, and those who are living won't die. In the days when you ate what was dead, you made it alive. When you're in the light, what will you do? On the day when you were one, you became divided. But when you become divided, what will you do?

SAYING XII.

James the Just will lead the disciples.

he disciples said to Jesus, We know you're going to leave us. Who will lead us then?

Jesus said to them, Wherever you are, you'll go to James the Just, for whom heaven and earth came into being.

SAYING XIII.

Thomas' confession.

esus asked his disciples, If you were to compare me to someone, who would you say I'm like?

Simon Peter said to him, You're like a just angel.

Matthew said to him, You're like a wise philosopher.

Thomas said to him, Teacher, I'm completely unable to say whom you're like.

Jesus said, I'm not your teacher. Because you've drunk, you've become intoxicated by the bubbling spring I've measured out.

He took him aside and told him three things. When Thomas returned to his companions, they asked, What did Jesus say to you?

Thomas said to them, If I tell you one of the things he said to me, you'll pick up stones and cast them at me, and fire will come out of the stones and burn you up.

SAYING XIV.

Jesus gives his disciples instructions for public ministry.

esus said to them, If you fast, you'll bring guilt upon yourselves; and if you pray, you'll be condemned; and if you make donations, you'll harm your spirits.

If they welcome you when you enter any land and go around in the countryside, heal those who are sick among them and eat whatever they give you, because it's not what goes into your mouth that will defile you. What comes out of your mouth is what will defile you.

SAYING XV.

Whom to worship.

esus said, When you see the one who wasn't born of a woman, fall down on your face and worship that person. That's your Father.

SAYING XVI.

Jesus did not come to bring peace, but war.

esus said, Maybe people think that I've come to cast peace on the world, and they don't know that I've come to cast divisions on the earth: fire,

sword, and war. Where there are five in a house, there'll be three against two and two against three, father against son and son against father. They'll stand up and be one.

SAYING XVII.

Jesus' divine gift.

esus said, I'll give you what no eye has ever seen, no ear has ever heard, no hand has ever touched, and no human mind has ever thought.

SAYING XVIII.

The end will be where the beginning is.

he disciples said to Jesus, Tell us about our end. How will it come?

Jesus asked, Have you discovered the beginning so that you can look for the end? Because the end will be where the beginning is. Blessed is the one who will stand up in the beginning. They'll know the end, and won't taste death.

SAYING XIX.

Five trees in paradise.

esus said, Blessed is the one who came into being before coming into being. If you become my disciples and listen to my message, these stones will become your servants; because there are five trees in paradise which don't change in summer or winter, and their leaves don't fall. Whoever knows them won't taste death.

SAYING XX.

The parable of the mustard seed.

he disciples said to Jesus, Tell us what the kingdom of heaven can be compared to.

He said to them, It can be compared to a mustard seed. Though it's the smallest of all the seeds, when it falls on tilled soil it makes a plant so large that it shelters the birds of heaven.

SAYING XXI.

The parables of the field, the bandits, and the reaper.

ary asked Jesus, Whom are your disciples like?

He said, They're like little children living in a field which isn't theirs. When the owners of the field come, they'll say, Give our field back to us. They'll strip naked in front of them to let them have it and give them their field.

So I say that if the owner of the house realizes the bandit is coming, they'll watch out beforehand and won't let the bandit break into the house of their domain and steal their possessions. You, then, watch out for the world! Prepare to defend yourself so that the bandits don't attack you, because what you're expecting will come. May there be a wise person among you!

When the fruit ripened, the reaper came quickly, sickle in hand, and harvested it. Anyone who has ears to hear should hear!

SAYING XXII.

Making the two into one.

esus saw some little children nursing. He said to his disciples, These nursing children can be compared to those who enter the kingdom.

They asked him, Then we'll enter the kingdom as little children?

Jesus said to them, When you make the two into one, and make the inner like the outer and the outer like the inner, and the upper like the lower, and so make the male and the female a single one so that the male won't be male nor the female female; when you make eyes in the place of an eye, a hand in the place of a hand, a foot in the place of a foot, and an image in the place of an image; then you'll enter [the kingdom].

SAYING XXIII.

Those who are chosen.

esus said, I'll choose you, one out of a thousand and two out of ten thousand, and they'll stand as a single one.

SAYING XXIV.

Light exists within a person of light.

is disciples said, Show us the place where you are, because we need to look for it.

He said to them, Anyone who has ears to hear should hear! Light exists within a person of light, and they light up the whole world. If they don't shine, there's darkness.

SAYING XXV.

Love and protect your brother and sister.

esus said, Love your brother (and sister) as your own soul. Protect them like the pupil of your eye.

SAYING XXVI.

Take the beam out of your own eye.

esus said, You see the speck that's in your brother's (or sister's) eye, but you don't see the beam in your own eye. When you get the beam out of your own eye, then you'll be able to see clearly to get the speck out of your brother's (or sister's) eye.

SAYING XXVII.

Fast from the world and make the Sabbath into a Sabbath.

f you don't fast from the world, you won't find the kingdom. If you don't make the Sabbath into a Sabbath, you won't see the Father.

SAYING XXVIII.

The world is drunk.

esus said, I stood in the middle of the world and appeared to them in the flesh. I found them all drunk; I didn't find any of them thirsty. My soul ached for the children of humanity, because they were blind in their hearts and couldn't see. They came into the world empty and plan on leaving the world empty. Meanwhile, they're drunk. When they shake off their wine, then they'll repent.

SAYING XXIX.

The flesh, the spirit, and the body.

esus said, If the flesh came into existence because of spirit, that's amazing. If spirit came into existence because of the body, that's really amazing! But I'm amazed at how [such] great wealth has been placed in this poverty.

SAYING XXX.

Where there are three deities.

esus said, Where there are three deities, they're divine. Where there are two or one, I'm with them.

SAYING XXXI.

The prophet and the doctor.

esus said, No prophet is welcome in their own village. No doctor heals those who know them.

SAYING XXXII.

The city on a high mountain.

esus said, A city built and fortified on a high mountain can't fall, nor can it be hidden.

SAYING XXIII.

The parable of the lamp.

esus said, What you hear with one ear, listen to with both, then proclaim from your rooftops. No one lights a lamp and puts it under a basket or in a hidden place. Rather, they put it on the stand so that everyone who comes and goes can see its light.

SAYING XXXIV.

When someone who doesn't see leads someone who doesn't see.

esus said, If someone who doesn't see leads someone else who doesn't see, both of them fall into a pit.

SAYING XXXV.

The parable of binding the strong.

esus said, No one can break into the house of the strong and take it by force without tying the hands of the strong. Then they can loot the house.

SAYING XXXVI.

Don't be anxious.

esus said, Don't be anxious from morning to evening or from evening to morning about what you'll wear.

SAYING XXXVII.

Seeing Jesus.

is disciples asked, When will you appear to us? When will we see you?

Jesus said, When you strip naked without being ashamed, and throw your clothes on the ground and stomp on them as little children would, then [you'll] see the Son of the Living One and won't be afraid.

SAYING XXXVIII.

Finding Jesus.

esus said, Often you've wanted to hear this message that I'm telling you, and you don't have anyone else from whom to hear it. There will be days when you'll look for me, but you won't be able to find me.

SAYING XXXIX.

The keys of knowledge have been hidden.

esus said, The Pharisees and the scribes have taken the keys of knowledge and hidden them. They haven't entered, and haven't let others enter who wanted to. So be wise as serpents and innocent as doves.

SAYING XL.

The parable of the malnourished grapevine.

esus said, A grapevine has been planted outside of the Father. Since it's malnourished, it'll be pulled up by its root and destroyed.

SAYING XLI.

More and less.

esus said, Whoever has something in hand will be given more, but whoever doesn't have anything will lose even what little they do have.

SAYING XLII.

Passing by.

esus said, Become passersby.

SAYING XLIII.

The tree and the fruit.

is disciples asked him, Who are you to say these things to us?

You don't realize who I am from what I say to you, but you've become like those Jews who either love the tree but hate its fruit, or love the fruit but hate the tree.

SAYING XLIV.

Whoever blasphemes.

esus said, Whoever blasphemes the Father will be forgiven, and whoever blasphemes the Son will be forgiven, but whoever blasphemes the Holy Spirit will not be forgiven, neither on earth nor in heaven.

SAYING XLV.

Those who are good bring good things.

esus said, Grapes aren't harvested from thorns, nor are figs gathered from thistles, because they don't produce fruit. [A person who's good] brings good things out of their treasure, and a person who's [evil] brings evil things out of their evil treasure. They say evil things because their heart is full of evil.

SAYING XLVI.

Greater than John the Baptizer.

esus said, From Adam to John the Baptizer, no one's been born who's so much greater than John the Baptizer that they shouldn't avert their eyes. But I say that whoever among you will become a little child will know the kingdom and become greater than John.

SAYING XLVII.

The parables of divided loyalties, new wine in old wineskins, and a new patch on old cloth.

esus said, It's not possible for anyone to mount two horses or stretch two bows, and it's not possible for a servant to follow two leaders, because they'll respect one and despise the other.

No one drinks old wine and immediately wants to drink new wine. And new wine isn't put in old wineskins, because they'd burst. Nor is old wine put in new wineskins, because it'd spoil.

A new patch of cloth isn't sewn onto an old coat, because it'd tear apart.

SAYING XLVIII.

Making peace.

esus said, If two make peace with each other in a single house, they'll say to the mountain, Go away, and it will.

SAYING XLIX.

Blessed are those who are one.

esus said, Blessed are those who are one—those who are chosen, because you'll find the kingdom. You've come from there and will return there.

SAYING L.

Origin and identity.

esus said, If they ask you, Where do you come from? tell them, We've come from the light, the place where light came into being by itself, [established] itself, and appeared in their image.

If they ask you, Is it you? then say, We are its children, and we're chosen by our living Father.

If they ask you, What's the sign of your Father in you? then say, It's movement and rest.

SAYING LI.

The new world has already come.

is disciples asked him, When will the dead have rest, and when will the new world come?

He said to them, What you're looking for has already come, but you don't know it.

SAYING LII.

Twenty-four prophets in Israel.

is disciples said to him, Twenty-four prophets have spoken in Israel, and they all spoke of you.

He said to them, You've ignored the Living One right in front of you, and you've talked about those who are dead.

SAYING LIII.

The true circumcision in spirit.

is disciples asked him, Is circumcision useful, or not?

He said to them, If it were useful, parents would have children who are born circumcised. But the true circumcision in spirit has become profitable in every way.

SAYING LIV.

Blessed are those who are poor.

esus said, Blessed are those who are poor, for yours is the kingdom of heaven.

SAYING LV.

Taking up the cross.

esus said, Whoever doesn't hate their father and mother can't become my disciple, and whoever doesn't hate their brothers and sisters and take up their cross like I do isn't worthy of me.

SAYING LVI.

The world is a corpse.

esus said, Whoever has known the world has found a corpse. Whoever has found a corpse, of them the world isn't worthy.

SAYING LVII.

The parable of the weeds.

esus said, My Fathers' kingdom can be compared to someone who had [good] seed. Their enemy came by night and sowed weeds among the good seed. The person didn't let anyone pull out the weeds, but said, So that you don't pull out the wheat along with the weeds. On the day of the harvest, the weeds will be obvious. Then they'll be pulled out and burned.

SAYING LVIII.

Finding life.

esus said, Blessed is the person who's gone to a lot of trouble. They've found life.

SAYING LIX.

Look for the Living One.

esus said, Look for the Living One while you're still alive. If you die and then try to look for him, you won't be able to.

SAYING LX.

Don't become a corpse.

hey saw a Samaritan carrying a lamb to Judea. He asked his disciples, What do you think he's going to do with that lamb?

They said to him, He's going to kill it and eat it.

He said to them, While it's living, he won't eat it, but only after he kills it and it becomes a corpse.

They said, He can't do it any other way.

He said to them, You, too, look for a resting place, so that you won't become a corpse and be eaten.

SAYING LXI.

Jesus and Salome.

esus said, Two will rest on a couch. One will die, the other will live.

Salome asked, Who are you, Sir, to climb onto my couch and eat off my table as if you're from someone?

Jesus said to her, I'm the one who exists in equality. Some of what belongs to my Father was given to me.

I'm your disciple.

So I'm telling you, if someone is <equal>, they'll be full of light; but if they're divided, they'll be full of darkness.

SAYING LXII.

Worthy of Jesus' mysteries.

esus said, I tell my mysteries to [those who are worthy of my] mysteries. Don't let your left hand know what your right hand is doing.

SAYING LXIII.

The parable of the rich fool.

esus said, There was a rich man who had much money. He said, I'll use my money to sow, reap, plant, and fill my barns with fruit, so that I won't need anything. That's what he was thinking to himself, but he died that very night. Anyone who has ears to hear should hear!

SAYING LXIV.

The parable of the dinner party.

esus said, Someone was planning on having guests. When dinner was ready, he sent his servant to call the visitors.

The servant went to the first and said, My master invites you.

They said, Some merchants owe me money. They're coming tonight. I need to go and give them instructions. Excuse me from the dinner.

The servant went to another one and said, My master invites you.

They said, I've just bought a house and am needed for the day. I won't have time.

The servant went to another one and said, My master invites you.

They said, My friend is getting married and I'm going to make dinner. I can't come. Excuse me from the dinner.

The servant went to another one and said, My master invites you.

They said, I've just bought a farm and am going to collect the rent. I can't come. Excuse me.

The servant went back and said to the master, The ones you've invited to the dinner have excused themselves.

The master said to his servant, Go out to the roads and bring whomever you find so that they can have dinner.

Buyers and merchants won't [enter] the places of my Father.

SAYING LXV.

The parable of the sharecroppers.

e said, A [creditor] owned a vineyard. He leased it out to some sharecroppers to work it so he could collect its fruit.

He sent his servant so that the sharecroppers could give him the fruit of the vineyard. They seized his servant, beat him, and nearly killed him.

The servant went back and told his master. His master said, Maybe he just didn't know them. He sent another servant, but the tenants beat that one too.

Then the master sent his son, thinking, Maybe they'll show some respect to my son.

Because they knew that he was the heir of the vineyard, the sharecroppers seized and killed him. Anyone who has ears to hear should hear!

SAYING LXVI.

The rejected cornerstone.

esus said, Show me the stone the builders rejected; that's the cornerstone.

SAYING LXVII.

Knowing isn't everything.

esus said, Whoever knows everything, but is personally lacking, lacks everything.

SAYING LXVIII.

Blessed are those who are persecuted.

esus said, Blessed are you when you're hated and persecuted, and no place will be found where you've been persecuted.

SAYING LXIX.

Blessed are those who are persecuted in their own hearts.

esus said, Blessed are those who've been persecuted in their own hearts. They've truly known the Father. Blessed are those who are hungry, so that their stomachs may be filled.

SAYING LXX.

Salvation is within.

esus said, If you give birth to what's within you, what you have within you will save you. If you don't have that within [you,] what you don't have within you [will] kill you.

SAYING LXXI.

Jesus will destroy the Temple.

esus said, I'll destroy [this] house, and no one will be able to build it [again.]

SAYING LXXII.

Jesus is not a divider.

omeone said to him], Tell my brothers to divide our inheritance with me.

He asked him, Who made me a divider?

He turned to his disciples and asked them, Am I really a divider?

SAYING LXXIII.

Workers for the harvest.

esus said, The harvest really is plentiful, but the workers are few. So pray that the Lord will send workers to the harvest.

SAYING LXXIV.

The well is empty.

e said, Lord, many are gathered around the well, but there's nothing to drink.

SAYING LXXV.

Entering the bridal chamber.

esus said, Many are waiting at the door, but those who are one will enter the bridal chamber.

SAYING LXXVI.

The parable of the pearl.

esus said, The Father's kingdom can be compared to a merchant with merchandise who found a pearl. The merchant was wise; they sold their merchandise and bought that single pearl for themselves.

You, too, look for the treasure that doesn't perish but endures, where no moths come to eat and no worms destroy.

SAYING LXXVII.

Jesus is everything.

esus said, I'm the light that's over everything. I am everything. Everything has come from me and unfolds toward me.

Split a log; I'm there. Lift the stone, and you'll find me there.

SAYING LXXVIII.

Into the desert.

esus asked, What did you go out into the desert to see? A reed shaken by the wind? A [person] wearing fancy clothes, [like your] rulers and powerful people? They (wear) fancy [clothes,] but can't know the Truth.

SAYING LXXXIX.

Blessed are those who have listened to the Father's message and kept it.

 woman in the crowd said to him, Blessed is the womb that bore you, and the breasts that nourished you.

He said to [her,] Blessed are those who have listened to the message of the Father and kept it, because there will be days when you'll say, Blessed is the womb that didn't conceive and the breasts that haven't given milk.

SAYING LXXX.

The world is a body.

 esus said, Whoever has known the world has found the body; but whoever has found the body, of them the world isn't worthy.

SAYING LXXXI.

Riches and renunciation.

 esus said, Whoever has become rich should become a ruler, and whoever has power should renounce it.

SAYING LXXXII.

Jesus and fire.

 esus said, Whoever is near me is near the fire, and whoever is far from me is far from the kingdom.

SAYING LXXXIII.

Images and light.

 esus said, Images are revealed to people, but the light within them is hidden in the image of the Father's light. He'll be revealed, but his image will be hidden by his light.

SAYING LXXXIV.

Previous images.

 esus said, When you see your likeness, you rejoice. But when you see your images that came into being before you did—which don't die, and aren't revealed—how much you'll have to bear!

SAYING LXXXV.

Adam wasn't worthy.

 esus said, Adam came into being from a great power and great wealth, but he didn't become worthy of you. If he had been

worthy, [he wouldn't have tasted] death.

SAYING LXXXVI.

Foxes, birds, and the Son of Humanity.

esus said, [The foxes have dens] and the birds have nests, but the Son of Humanity has nowhere to lay his head and rest.

SAYING LXXXVII.

Body and soul.

esus said, How miserable is the body that depends on a body, and how miserable is the soul that depends on both.

SAYING LXXXVIII.

Angels and prophets.

esus said, The angels and the prophets will come to you and give you what belongs to you. You'll give them what you have and ask yourselves, When will they come and take what is theirs?

SAYING LXXXIX.

Inside and outside.

esus asked, Why do you wash the outside of the cup? Don't you know that whoever created the inside created the outside too?

SAYING XC.

Jesus' yoke is easy.

esus said, Come to me, because my yoke is easy and my requirements are light. You'll be refreshed.

SAYING XCI.

Reading the signs.

hey said to him, Tell us who you are so that we may believe in you.

He said to them, You read the face of the sky and the earth, but you don't know the one right in front of you, and you don't know how to read the present moment.

SAYING XCII.

Look and find.

esus said, Look and you'll find. I didn't answer your questions before. Now I want to

give you answers, but you aren't looking for them.

SAYING XCIII.

Don't throw pearls to the pigs.

on't give what's holy to the dogs, or else it might be thrown on the manure pile. Don't throw pearls to the pigs, or else they might grind it [to bits.]

SAYING XCIV.

Knock and it will be opened.

esus [said,] Whoever looks will find, [and whoever knocks,] it will be opened for them.

SAYING XCV.

Giving money.

esus said,] If you have money, don't lend it at interest. Instead, give [it to] someone from whom you won't get it back.

SAYING XCVI.

The parable of the yeast.

esus [said,] The Father's kingdom can be compared to a woman who took a little yeast and [hid] it in flour. She made it into large loaves of bread. Anyone who has ears to hear should hear!

SAYING XCVII.

The parable of the woman carrying a jar of flour.

esus said, The Father's kingdom can be compared to a woman carrying a jar of flour. While she was walking down [a] long road, the jar's handle broke and the flour spilled out behind her on the road. She didn't know it, and didn't realize there was a problem until she got home, put down the jar, and found it empty.

SAYING XCVIII.

The parable of the assassin.

esus said, The Father's kingdom can be compared to a man who wanted to kill someone powerful. He drew his sword in his house and drove it into the wall to figure out whether his hand was strong enough. Then he killed the powerful one.

Albrecht Altdorfer, Christ Taking Leave of His Mother
ca. 1513, Metropolitan Museum of Art

SAYING XCIX.

Jesus' brothers, sisters, and mother.

he disciples said to him, Your brothers (and sisters) and mother are standing outside.

He said to them, The people here who do the will of my Father are my brothers (and sisters) and mother; they're the ones who will enter my Father's kingdom.

SAYING C.

Give to Caesar what belongs to Caesar.

hey showed Jesus a gold coin and said to him, Those who belong to Caesar demand tribute from us.

He said to them, Give to Caesar what belongs to Caesar, give to God what belongs to God, and give to me what belongs to me.

SAYING CI.

Becoming Jesus' disciple.

hoever doesn't hate their [father] and mother as I do can't become my [disciple,] and whoever [doesn't] love their [father] and mother as I do can't become my [disciple.] For my mother [...,] but [my] true [Mother] gave me Life.

SAYING CII.

Like a dog in the feeding trough.

esus said, Woe to the Pharisees who are like a dog sleeping in a feeding trough for cattle, because the dog doesn't eat, and [doesn't let] the cattle eat either.

SAYING CIII.

The parable of the bandits.

esus said, Blessed is the one who knows where the bandits are going to enter. [They can] get up to assemble their defenses and be prepared to defend themselves before they arrive.

SAYING CIV.

Prayer and fasting.

hey said to [Jesus,] Come, let's pray and fast today.

Jesus asked, What sin have I committed? Have I failed?

Rather, when the groom leaves the bridal chamber, then people should fast and pray.

SAYING CV.

Knowing father and mother.

esus said, Whoever knows their father and mother will be called a bastard.

SAYING CVI.

Becoming Children of Humanity.

esus said, When you make the two into one, you'll become Children of Humanity, and if you say Mountain, go away!, it'll go.

SAYING CVII.

The parable of the lost sheep.

esus said, The kingdom can be compared to a shepherd who had a hundred sheep. The largest one strayed. He left the ninety-nine and looked for that one until he found it. Having gone through the trouble, he said to the sheep: I love you more than the ninety-nine.

SAYING CVIII.

Becoming like Jesus.

esus said, Whoever drinks from my mouth will become like me, and I myself will become like them; then, what's hidden will be revealed to them.

SAYING CIX.

The parable of the hidden treasure.

esus said, The kingdom can be compared to someone who had a treasure [hidden] in their field. [They] didn't know about it. After they died, they left it to their son. The son didn't know it either. He took the field and sold it.

The buyer plowed the field, [found] the treasure, and began to loan money at interest to whomever they wanted.

SAYING CX.

Renouncing the world.

esus said, Whoever has found the world and become rich should renounce the world.

SAYING CXI.

Those who won't see death.

esus said, The heavens and the earth will roll up in front of you, and whoever lives from the Living One won't see death.

Doesn't Jesus say, Whoever finds themselves, of them the world isn't worthy?

SAYING CXII.

The flesh and the soul.

esus said, Woe to the flesh that depends on the soul. Woe to the soul that depends on the flesh.

SAYING CXIII.

The kingdom is already present.

is disciples asked him, When will the kingdom come?

It won't come by looking for it. They won't say, Look over here! or, Look over there! Rather, the Father's kingdom is already spread out over the earth, and people don't see it.

SAYING CXIV.

Peter and Mary.

imon Peter said to them, Mary should leave us, because women aren't worthy of life.

Jesus asked, Look, am I to make her a man? So that she may become a living spirit too, she's equal to you men, because every woman who makes herself manly will enter the kingdom of heaven.

The Gospel According to Thomas.

THE GOSPEL OF PHILIP

he only known copy of the Gospel of Philip is a fourth-century Egyptian version discovered in a library of books unearthed in 1945. It immediately follows the Gospel of Thomas in the same volume. For more information, see my book, *The Gospel of Philip: The Divine Mysteries of Marriage and Rebirth,* published in 2017.

This is not a narrative Gospel, but rather a dense series of reflections on the life and death of Jesus. Heavily influenced by Syriac Christianity, it's noteworthy for its sacramental theology and mystical reflections on marriage. As an esoteric text, this Gospel is intentionally opaque, inviting readers to ponder its meanings, puns, wordplays, and paradoxes.

CHAP. I.

Gentiles, Hebrews, and Christians.

 Hebrew creates a Hebrew, and [those] of this kind are called a proselyte. But a [proselyte] doesn't create (another) proselyte. They're like [...] and they create others [...] **52** it's good enough for them that they come into being.

The slave seeks only freedom; they don't seek their master's property. But the son isn't just a son; he claims his father's inheritance for himself. Those who inherit the dead are themselves dead, and they inherit the dead. Those who inherit the living are themselves alive, and they inherit (both) the living and the dead. The dead can't inherit anything, because how can the dead inherit? If the dead inherits the living they won't die, but the dead will live even more! A gentile doesn't die, because they've never lived in order that they may die. Whoever has believed in the Truth has lived, and is at risk of dying, because they're alive since the day Christ came. The world is created, the cities adorned, and the dead carried out.

When we were Hebrews, we were fatherless—we had (only) our mother. But when we became Christians, we gained both father and mother.

CHAP. II.

Sow in the world to reap in the summer. Christ laid down his life and took it up. Light and darkness are twins.

hose who sow in the winter reap in the summer. The winter is the world, the summer the other age. Let's sow in the world so that we may reap in the summer. Because of this, it's not right for us to pray in the winter. The summer follows the winter. But if someone reaps in the winter they won't reap, but uproot, as this kind won't produce fruit [...] it doesn't just come out [...] but in the other Sabbath [...] it's fruitless.

Christ came **53** to buy some, but to save others, and to redeem yet others. He bought those who were strangers, made them his own, and set them apart as a pledge as he wanted to. It wasn't just when he appeared that he laid down his life when he wanted to, but since the day the world came into being he laid down his life when he wanted to. Then he came first to take it, since it had been pledged. It was dominated by the robbers that had captured it, but he saved it; and those who are good in the world he redeemed, as well as those who are bad.

The light and the darkness, the right and the left, are twins. They're inseparable. So, those who are good aren't good, those who are bad aren't bad, nor is life (really) life, nor is death (really) death. Because of this, each one will be dissolved into its origin from the beginning. But those who are exalted above the world are indissoluble and eternal.

CHAP. III.

Worldly names deceive. The name which the Father gave the Son is exalted over everything. There's only one Truth, but it's many things for us.

he names that are given to those who are worldly are very deceptive, because they turn the heart away from what's right to what's not right, and

someone who hears God doesn't think of what's right but thinks of what's not right. So also with the Father, the Son, the Holy Spirit, the life, the light, the resurrection, the church, and all the others—they don't think of [what's right] but think of what's [not] right, [unless] they've learned what's right. The [names that were heard] exist in the world [...] **54** [deceive. If they existed] in the (eternal) age they wouldn't have been used as names in the world, nor would they have been placed among worldly things. They have an end in the (eternal) age.

There's one name that isn't uttered in the world: the name which the Father gave to the Son. It's exalted over everything; it's the Father's name, because the Son wouldn't have become father unless he had taken the name of the Father. Those who have this name know it, but don't say it; and those who don't have it, don't know it. But Truth brought names into the world for us, because it's impossible for us to learn (Truth) without these names. There's only one Truth, but it's many things for us, to teach this one thing in love through many things.

CHAP. IV.

The Rulers deceive and enslave humanity. Animals are sacrificed to animals. Christ brought bread from heaven so humans wouldn't have to eat like animals. Truth is sown everywhere, but few see it reaped.

The rulers wanted to deceive humanity, because (the rulers) saw that (humanity) had a kinship with those that are truly good. They took the name of those that are good and gave it to those that aren't good, to deceive (humanity) by the names and bind them to those that aren't good; and then, what a favor they do for them! They take them from those that aren't good and place them among those that are good. They knew what they were doing, because they wanted to take those who were free and place them in slavery forever. There are powers that exist [...] humanity, not wanting them to be [saved,] so that they may be [...] because if humanity [was saved,] sacrifices [wouldn't] happen [...] and animals offered **55** up to the powers, because those to whom offerings were made were animals.

They were offered up alive, but when they were offered up they died. A human was offered up to God dead, and he lived.

Before Christ came, there wasn't any bread in the world—just as Paradise, where Adam was, had many trees to feed the animals but no wheat to feed humanity. Humanity used to eat like the animals, but when Christ, the perfect human, came, he brought bread from heaven so that humanity would be fed with the food of humanity.

The rulers thought they did what they did by their own power and will, but the Holy Spirit was secretly accomplishing everything it wanted to through them. Truth, which has existed from the beginning, is sown everywhere; and many see it being sown, but few see it being reaped.

CHAP. V.

Mary did not conceive by the Holy Spirit. The Lord had two fathers. Christ has everything within himself.

ome say that Mary conceived by the Holy Spirit. They're wrong; they don't know what they're saying. When did a woman ever conceive by a woman? Mary is the virgin whom no power defiled. This is the great testimony of those Hebrews who became (the first) apostles and (the) apostolic (successors). The virgin whom no power defiled [...] the powers defiled themselves.

And the Lord [wouldn't] have said, my [Father who is in] heaven unless [he] had another father. Instead, he would simply have said [my Father.] The Lord said to the [disciples, ...] **56** [from] every [house] and bring into the Father's house, but don't steal (anything) from the Father's house or carry it away.

Jesus is a hidden name; Christ is a revealed name. So Jesus is not translated, but he's called by his name Jesus. But the name Christ in Syriac is Messiah, in Greek Christ, and all the others have it according to their own language. The Nazarene reveals what's hidden. Christ has everything within himself, whether human or angel or mystery, and the Father.

CHAP. VI.

Resurrection precedes death. The soul is a great and valuable thing. Flesh and blood won't inherit God's kingdom. Everything is purified by water and fire.

hose who say that the Lord died first and then arose are wrong, because he arose first and (then) he died. Anyone who doesn't first acquire the resurrection won't die. As God lives, that one would <die>!

No one will hide something great and valuable in a great thing, but often someone has put countless thousands into something worth (only) a penny. It's the same with the soul; a valuable thing came to be in a contemptible body.

Some are afraid that they'll arise naked. So they want to arise in the flesh, and [they] don't know that those who wear the [flesh] are naked. Those [...] to strip themselves naked [are] not naked. Flesh [and blood won't] inherit [God's] kingdom. What is it that **57** won't inherit? That which is on us. But what is it, too, that will inherit? It is Jesus' (flesh) and blood. Because of this, he said, Whoever doesn't eat my flesh and drink my blood doesn't have life in them. What's his flesh? It's the Word, and his blood is the Holy Spirit. Whoever has received these have food, drink, and clothing.

(So) I myself disagree with the others who say, It won't arise. Both (sides) are wrong. You who say, the flesh won't arise, tell me what will arise, so that we may honor you. You say, the spirit in the flesh and this other light in the flesh. (But) this saying is in the flesh too, because whatever you say, you can't say apart from the flesh. It's necessary to arise in this flesh, since everything exists in it. In this world, people are better than the clothes they wear. In the kingdom of heaven, the clothes are better than the people who wear them.

Everything is purified by water and fire—the visible by the visible, the hidden by the hidden. Some things are hidden by things that are visible. There's water in water, and fire in chrism.

CHAP. VII.

Jesus appeared to all as they'd be able to see him. Unite with the images. The Lamb is the key to the door. Heavenly children outnumber earthly children. Only fathers (i.e., priests) can beget (spiritual) children. The Lord traveled with three

Marys. The Holy Spirit tricks evil powers into working for the holy ones. Offerings aren't acceptable without salt. Echamoth is the greater Wisdom and Echmoth the lesser.

esus took all of them by stealth, because he didn't appear as he was, but he appeared as [they'd] be able to see him. He appeared to them (in) [all these] (ways): he [appeared] to [the] great as great. He [appeared] to the small as small. He [appeared] **58** [to the] angels as an angel, and to humans as a human. So his Word hid itself from everyone. Some did see him, thinking they were seeing themselves. But when he appeared to his disciples in glory on the mountain, he wasn't small. He became great, but he made the disciples great (too) so that they would be able to see him as great.

He said on that day in the Eucharist, You who've united the perfect light with the Holy Spirit, unite the angels with us too, with the images!

Don't despise the Lamb, because without him it's impossible to see the door. No one will be able to approach the king naked.

The children of the heavenly human are more numerous than those of the earthly human. If Adam has so many children, even though they die, how many children does the perfect human have—those who don't die, but are begotten all the time?

The father makes a son, but it's impossible for a son to make a son, because it's impossible for someone who's been born to beget (children); the son begets brothers (and sisters), not sons. All who are begotten in the world are begotten physically, and the others in [...] are begotten by him [...] out there to the human [...] in the [...] heavenly place [...] it from the mouth [...] the Word came out from there **59** they would be nourished from the mouth [and] become perfect. The perfect are conceived and begotten through a kiss. Because of this we kiss each other too, conceiving from the grace within each other.

There were three who traveled with the Lord all the time: His mother Mary, her sister, and Magdalene, who is called his companion; because Mary is his sister, his mother, and his partner.

The Father and the Son are single names; the Holy Spirit

is a double name, because they're everywhere. They're in heaven, they're below, they're hidden, and they're revealed. The Holy Spirit is revealed below and hidden in heaven.

Those who are holy are served through the evil powers, because the Holy Spirit has blinded them so that they think they're serving a (regular) human when they're (really) working for the holy ones. So a disciple asked the Lord one day about a worldly thing. He told him, Ask your Mother, and she'll give you from someone else.

The apostles said to the disciples, May our entire offering acquire salt. They called [...] salt. Without it, the offering doesn't [become] acceptable. But Wisdom [is] childless; because of this [she's] called [...] this of salt, the place they'll [...] in their own way. The Holy Spirit [...] **60** [...] many children.

What belongs to the father belongs to the son, and he himself—the son—as long as he's little, is not entrusted with what's his. When he becomes a man, his father gives him everything that belongs to him.

Those who've been begotten by the Spirit and go astray, go astray through it too. Because of this, through this one Spirit it blazes, that is, the fire, and it's extinguished.

Echamoth is one thing and Echmoth another. Echamoth is simply Wisdom, but Echmoth is the Wisdom of Death, which knows death. This is called the Little Wisdom.

CHAP. VIII.

The Holy Spirit rules all the powers. Partnership between those who are dissimilar is unfaithfulness.

here are animals that submit to humans, like the calf, the donkey, and others of this kind. Others are not submissive, and live alone in the wilderness. Humanity ploughs the field with the submissive animals, and consequently nourishes itself and the animals, whether submissive or not. That's what it's like with the perfect human: they plough with the submissive powers, preparing for everyone that will exist. So because of this the whole place stands, whether the good or the evil, and the right and the left. The Holy Spirit shepherds everyone and rules all the powers—

those that are submissive, those that [aren't], and those that are alone—because truly it [...] confines them [so that ...] want to, they won't be able to [leave.]

[The one who's been] formed [is beautiful, but] you'd find his children being **61** noble forms. If he weren't formed but begotten, you'd find that his offspring was noble. But now he was formed, and he begot. What nobility is this? First there was unfaithfulness, and then murder; and (Cain) was begotten in unfaithfulness, because he was the son of the serpent. Because of this he became a murderer like his father too, and he killed his brother (Abel). Every partnership between those who are dissimilar is unfaithfulness.

CHAP. IX.

God is a dyer. You become what you see. Faith receives and love gives. The meaning of Jesus the Nazarene Messiah. God's children are valuable. God is a human-eater. The making and breaking of glass and pottery. Many people travel, but don't get anywhere. The Eucharist is Jesus. The Lord dyes seventy-two colors white.

God is a dyer. Like the good dyes—they're called true—die with what's been dyed in them, so it is with those who were dyed by God. Because his dyes are immortal, they become immortal by means of his colors. But God baptizes in water.

It's impossible for anyone to see anything that really exists unless they become like them. It's not like the person in the world who sees the sun without becoming a sun, and who sees heaven and earth and everything else without becoming them. That's the way it is. But you've seen something of that place, and have become them. You saw the Spirit, you became spirit; you saw Christ, you became Christ; you saw [the Father, you] will become father. Because of this, [here] you see everything and don't [see yourself,] but you see yourself [there,] because you'll [become] what you see.

Faith receives; love gives. [No one will be able to] **62** [receive] without faith, and no one will be able to give without love. So we believe in order that we may receive, but we give in order that we may love, since anyone who doesn't give with love doesn't get anything out of it. Whoever hasn't received the Lord is still a Hebrew.

The apostles before us called (him) Jesus the Nazarene Messiah, that is, Jesus the Nazarene Christ. The last name is Christ, the first is Jesus, the middle one is the Nazarene. Messiah has two meanings: both Christ and the measured. Jesus in Hebrew is the redemption. Nazara is the Truth. So the Nazarene is the Truth. Christ is the one who was measured. The Nazarene and Jesus are the ones who were measured.

A pearl doesn't become less valuable if it's cast down into the mud, nor will it become more valuable if it's anointed with balsam; but it's valuable to its owner all the time. That's what it's like with God's children: no matter where they are, they're still valuable to their Father.

If you say, I'm a Jew, no one will be moved. If you say, I'm a Roman, no one will be disturbed. If you say, I'm a Greek, a Barbarian, a slave, [a free person,] no one will be troubled. [If] you [say,] I'm a Christian, the [...] will tremble. If only [... of] this kind, this one [who ...] won't be able to endure [hearing] his name.

God is a human-eater. **63** Because of this, the human is [sacrificed] to him. Before the human was sacrificed, animals were sacrificed, because those to whom they were sacrificed weren't gods.

Vessels of glass and pottery come into being by means of fire. But if glass vessels break they're remade, because they came into being by means of a breath, but if pottery vessels break they're destroyed, because they came into being without breath.

A donkey turning a millstone traveled a hundred miles. When it was released, it still found itself in the same place. Many people travel, but don't get anywhere. When evening came, they saw neither city nor village, nor anything created nor natural, nor power nor angel. The wretches worked in vain.

The Eucharist is Jesus, because in Syriac he's called Pharisatha, that is, the one who's spread out, because Jesus came to crucify the world.

The Lord went into Levi's place of dyeing. He took seventy-two colors and threw them into the vat. He brought all of them out white and said,

Virgilius Solis, 1524-1562, The Baptism of Christ
Rijksmuseum

That's the way the Son of Humanity has come [as] a dyer.

CHAP. X.

Jesus loved Mary Magdalene. Humanity is superior. Receiving the Holy Spirit. The mystery of marriage is great. The only way to escape impure spirits is by receiving a male power and a female power in the bridal chamber.

he Wisdom who is called the barren is the Mother [of the angels] and [the] companion of the [… Mary] Magdalene [… loved her] more than the disciples [… he] kissed her on her [… many] times. The rest of […] **64** […] they asked him, Why do you love her more than all of us? In response the Savior said to them, Why don't I love you like her? When a person who doesn't see and one who does are both in the dark, they're no different from one another. When the light comes, the one who sees will see the light, and the one who doesn't see will remain in the dark.

The Lord said, Blessed is the one who exists before existing, because they who exist did exist, and will exist.

The superiority of humanity isn't revealed, but exists in what's hidden. So (humanity) masters animals that are stronger, that are greater in terms of that which is revealed and that which is hidden. This allows them to survive; but if humanity separates from (the animals), they kill, bite, and eat each other, because they didn't find food. But now they've found food because humanity has worked the earth.

If someone goes down into the water and comes up without having received anything, and says, I'm a Christian, they've borrowed the name at interest. But if they receive the Holy Spirit, they have the gift of the name. Whoever has received a gift doesn't have it taken away, but whoever has borrowed it at interest has to give it back. That's what it's like when someone comes into being in a mystery.

[The] mystery of marriage [is] great, because [without] it the world would [not exist;] because [the] structure of [the world …] but the structure [… the marriage.] Think about the [intimate …] defiled, because it has […] power. Its image **65** exists in a [defilement.]

The impure spirits take male and female [forms]. The males are those that are intimate with the souls which dwell in a female form, and the females are those that mingle with those in a male form through disobedience. No one will be able to escape being bound by them without receiving a male power and a female one—the groom and the bride—in the image of the bridal chamber. When the foolish females see a male sitting alone, they jump on him, play with him, and defile him. In the same way, when the foolish males see a beautiful female sitting alone, they seduce and coerce her, wanting to defile her. But if they see the husband and his wife sitting together, the females can't go inside the husband, nor the males inside the wife. That's what it's like when the image unites with the angel; no one will be able to dare to go inside the [male] or the female.

CHAP. XI.

Overcoming the world. The middle is death. The offspring of the bridal chamber was from water, fire, and light. Truth didn't come into the world naked, but it came in types and images. The Lord did everything in a mystery: A baptism, a chrism, a Eucharist, a redemption, a bridal chamber. Pray in private. Christ brought out those who entered and brought in those who went out.

hoever comes out of the world can no longer be bound because they were in the world. They're revealed to be above the desire of the [… and] fear. They're master over […] they're better than envy. If […] come, they (the powers) bind and choke [them.] How will [they] be able to escape the [great powers …]? How will they be able to […]? There are some who [say,] We're faithful, in order that […] **66** [impure spirit] and demon, because if they had the Holy Spirit, no impure spirit would cling to them. Don't fear the flesh, nor love it. If you fear it, it'll master you; if you love it, it'll swallow and choke you.

Someone exists either in this world, or in the resurrection, or in the middle places. May I never be found there! There's both good and evil in this world. Its good things aren't good, and its evil things aren't evil. But there's an evil after this world which is truly evil: that which is called the middle. It's death. While we're in this world, it's right for us to acquire the resurrection for ourselves, so that when we're stripped of the flesh we'll be found in the rest and not travel in the middle, because many stray on the way.

It's good to come out of the world before one sins. There are some who neither want to nor can, but others who, if they wanted to, (still) wouldn't benefit, because they didn't act. The wanting makes them sinners. But (even) if they don't want, justice will (still) be hidden from them. It's not the will, and it's not the act.

An apostle saw [in a] vision some people confined in a burning house, and bound with burning […] thrown […] of the burning […] them in […] and they said to them [… able] to be saved […] they didn't want to, and they received […] punishment, which is called **67** the [outer] darkness, because it […]

The soul and the spirit came into being from water and fire. The offspring of the bridal chamber was from water and fire and light. The fire is the chrism, the light is the fire. I'm not talking about that formless fire, but of the other one whose form is white, which is bright and beautiful, and which gives beauty.

Truth didn't come into the world naked, but it came in types and images. (The world) won't receive it in any other way. There's a rebirth, and an image of rebirth. It's truly necessary to be begotten again through the image. What's the resurrection and the image? Through the image it's necessary for it to arise. The bridal chamber and the image? Through the image it's necessary for them to enter the Truth, which is the restoration. It's not only necessary for those who acquire the name of the Father and the Son and the Holy Spirit, but they too have been acquired for you. If someone doesn't acquire them, the name will also be taken from them. But they're received in the chrism of the […] of the power of the cross. The apostles called this [the] right and the left, because this person is no longer a [Christian,] but a Christ.

The Lord [did] everything in a mystery: a baptism, a chrism, a Eucharist, a redemption, a bridal chamber

[…] he [said,] I came to make [the below] like the [above and the outside] like the [inside, and to unite] them in the place. […] here through [types …] Those who say […] there's one above […, they're wrong, because] what's revealed **68** is that […] that [which] is known as what's below, and what's hidden is to it what's above it, because it's good, and they talk about the inside and what's outside and what's outside the outside. So the Lord called destruction the outer darkness. There's nothing outside it.

He said, My Father who's hidden. He said, Enter your closet, shut the door behind you, and pray to your Father who's hidden, that is, the one who's within all of them. But the one who's within all of them is the fullness. Beyond that, there's nothing else within. This is what's called that which is above them.

Before Christ, some came from where they were no longer able to enter, and they went where they were no longer able to come out. Then Christ came. He brought out those who entered, and brought in those who went out.

CHAP. XII.

Death came into being when Adam and Eve separated. Jesus was divided on the cross. A bridal chamber is for free people and virgins. When we were begotten, we were united. It's necessary to baptize in both water and chrism (i.e., holy anointing oil). There were three houses of offering in Jerusalem. The powers can't bind those who have put on the perfect light. Christ came to repair the separation of female and male by uniting the two again. In Jesus' baptism in the Jordan River, the Father (i.e., the groom, or the Word) and the virgin (i.e., the bride, or the Spirit) became Jesus' flesh and blood, respectively, which, when received in the Eucharist, unites disciples with the body of Christ. Adam came into being from two virgins, and Christ was begotten from a (spiritual) virgin to rectify the fall. There are two trees growing in Paradise. The children of the bridal chamber will be named Rest.

hen Eve was [in] Adam, death didn't

Albrecht Altdorfer, The Crucifixion, ca. 1513
Metropolitan Museum of Art

exist. When she separated from him, death came into being. If he [enters] again and receives it for himself, there will be no death.

[My] God, my God, why, Lord, [have] you forsaken me? He said this on the cross, because he was divided in that place. […] that he was begotten through that which […] from God. The […] from the dead […] exists, but […] he's perfect […] of flesh, but this […] is true flesh […] isn't true, [but …] image of the true.

69 A bridal chamber isn't for the animals, nor for the slaves, nor for the impure, but it's for free people and virgins.

We're begotten again through the Holy Spirit, but we're begotten through Christ by two things. We're anointed through the Spirit. When we were begotten, we were united.

Without light, no one can see themselves in water or in a mirror; nor again will you be able to see in light without water or mirror. Because of this, it's necessary to baptize in both: in the light and in the water, but the light is the chrism.

There were three houses of offering in Jerusalem. The one which opens to the west is called the Holy. The other one, which opens to the south, is called the Holy of the Holy. The third, which opens to the east, is called the Holy of the Holies, the place where the high priest enters alone. Baptism is the Holy house. [Redemption] is the Holy of the Holy. The [Holy] of the Holies is the bridal chamber. The [baptism] includes the resurrection [with] the redemption. The redemption is in the bridal chamber. But [the] bridal chamber is better than […] You won't find its […] those who pray […] Jerusalem. […] Jerusalem who [… Jerusalem,] being seen […] these that are called [the Holies] of the Holies [… the] veil torn […] bridal chamber except the image [… which] **70** [is above. So] its veil was torn from top to bottom, because it was necessary for some from below to go up above.

The powers can't see those who have put on the perfect light, and they can't bind them. But one will put on that light in the mystery of the union.

If the female wouldn't have been separated from the male, she wouldn't have died with the male. His separation was the beginning of death. Because of this, Christ came to repair the separation that existed since the beginning by uniting the two again. He'll give life to those who died as a result of the separation by uniting them. Now, the wife unites with her husband in the bridal chamber, and those who have united in the bridal chamber won't be separated any longer. Because of this, Eve separated from Adam, because she didn't unite with him in the bridal chamber.

It was through a breath that Adam's soul came into being. Its partner was the spirit. That which was given to him was his mother. His soul was [taken] and he was given [life] (Eve) in its place. When he was united [...] words that were better than the powers, and they envied him [...] spiritual partner [...] hidden [...] that is, the [...] themselves [...] bridal chamber so that [...] Jesus appeared [... the] Jordan, the [fullness of the kingdom] of heaven. He who [was begotten] before everything **71** was begotten again. He [who was anointed] first was anointed again. He who was redeemed, redeemed again.

If it's necessary to speak of a mystery: the Father of everything united with the virgin who came down, and a fire enlightened (Jesus) on that day. He revealed the great bridal chamber, so his body came into being on that day. He came out of the bridal chamber like the one who came into being from the groom and the bride. That's the way Jesus established everything within himself. It's also necessary for each of the disciples to enter into his rest through these things.

Adam came into being from two virgins: from the Spirit and from the virgin earth. So Christ was begotten from a virgin, to rectify the fall that occurred in the beginning.

There are two trees growing in Paradise. One begets [animals,] the other begets humans. Adam [ate] from the tree that begot animals, [and he] became an animal, and he begot [animals.] So Adam's children worship the [animals.] The tree [...] is fruit [...] this they [...] ate the [...] fruit of the [...] beget humans [...] of the human of [...] God makes the human, [... humans] make [God.] **72** That's what it's like in the world: humans make gods and worship their creation. It would be better for the gods to worship humans!

The truth is that the work of humankind comes from their

power, so they're called the powers. Their works are their children, who come into being through rest; so their power exists in their works, but the rest is revealed in their children. And you'll find that this extends to the image. And this is the person in the image: they do their works through their power, but they beget their children through rest.

In this world, the slaves work for the free. In the kingdom of heaven, the free will serve the slaves. The children of the bridal chamber will serve the children of the [marriage. The] children of the bridal chamber have a [single] name: Rest. [Being] together they don't need to take form, [because they have] contemplation [...] they're many [...] with those who are in the [...] the glories of the [...] not [...] them [...] go down to the [water ...] they'll redeem themselves [...] that is, those who have [...] in his name, because he said: [That's the way] we'll fulfill **73** all righteousness.

CHAP. XIII.

Resurrection precedes death. From the Tree of Life came the chrism and the resurrection. The Law was the tree of knowledge which created death for those who ate from it. The chrism is better than baptism. Whoever is anointed has everything: the resurrection, the light, the cross, the Holy Spirit. The world came into being through a transgression. The cup of prayer fills with the Holy Spirit. Like begins like. It's necessary for everyone who has everything to know themselves completely. The holy man (i.e., the priest) is completely holy. Whoever knows the Truth is a free person. Love the Lord. Like unites with like.

hose who say that they'll die first and (then) they'll rise are wrong. If they don't first receive the resurrection while they're living, they won't receive anything when they die. It's the same when they talk about baptism and they say baptism is a great thing, because those who receive it will live.

Philip the apostle said that Joseph the carpenter planted a garden because he needed wood for his trade. It was he who made the cross from the trees he planted, and his offspring hung from what he planted. His offspring was Jesus, and the plant was the cross. But the Tree of Life is in the middle of Paradise, and from the olive tree came the chrism, and from that the resurrection.

This world eats corpses. All that are eaten in it die also. Truth eats life, so no one nourished by [Truth] will die. Jesus came from that place, he brought food from there, and to those who wanted, he gave them [to eat, so that] they won't die.

[God ...] a Paradise, [human ...] Paradise, there are [...] and [...] of God [...] those in [it ...] I wish that [Paradise ...] they'll say to me, [... eat] this, or don't eat [that ...] **74** wish. The tree of knowledge is the place where I'll eat everything. It killed Adam, but here it makes humanity live. The Law was the tree. It has the power to give the knowledge of good and evil. It neither kept them from evil nor placed them in the good, but it created death for those who ate from it; because when it said, Eat this, don't eat that, it became the beginning of death.

The chrism is better than baptism, since we're called Christians because of the chrism, not because of baptism. And it was because of the chrism that Christ was named, because the Father anointed the Son, and the Son anointed the apostles, and the apostles anointed us. Whoever is anointed has everything: the resurrection, the light, the cross, the Holy Spirit. The Father gave this to him in the bridal chamber, and he received it. The Father was in the Son and the Son in the Father. This is [the kingdom] of heaven.

The Lord said [it] well: Some went to the kingdom of heaven laughing and they came out [...] a Christian [...] and as soon as [... went down] into the water and he [...] everything about [...] it's [a] game, [but ... disregard] this [...] to the kingdom of [heaven ...] if they disregard [...] and if they scorn it as a game, [... out] laughing. It's the same way **75** with the bread and the cup and the oil, though there's one better than these.

The world came into being through a transgression, because the one who created it wanted to create it imperishable and immortal. He fell away and didn't get what he wanted, because the world wasn't imperishable, and the one who created it wasn't imperishable; because things aren't imperishable, but rather children. None will be able to receive imperishability without becoming a child. But whoever can't receive, how much more will they be unable to give?

The cup of prayer has wine and water, since it's laid down as the type of the blood over which they give thanks. It fills with the Holy Spirit, and it belongs to the completely perfect human. Whenever we drink this, we'll receive the perfect human. The living water is a body. It's necessary for us to put on the living human. So coming down to the water, they strip themselves so that they'll put on that one.

A horse begets a horse, a human begets a human, and a god begets god. It's the same way with [the groom] and [brides too.] They [come into being] from the [...] No Jew [...] from [...] exists and [...] from the Jews [...] the Christians [...] called these [...] the chosen race of [...] **76** and the true humanity and the Son of Humanity and the offspring of the Son of Humanity. This true race is known in the world. These are the places where the children of the bridal chamber exist.

In this world, union is between male and female, the place of power and weakness; in the (eternal) age, the union is like something else, but we refer to them by the same names. There are other names, however, that are above every name that's named, and they're better than the strong, because where there's force, there are those who are even more powerful. They're not (two) different things, but they're both the same thing. This is what won't be able to come down upon the fleshly heart.

Isn't it necessary for everyone who has everything to know themselves completely? Some who don't know themselves won't be able to enjoy what they have, but those who've come to understand themselves will enjoy them.

Not only won't they be able to bind the perfect human, they won't be able to see them (the perfect human), because if they see them they'll bind them. There's no other way for someone to acquire this grace for themselves [except by] putting on the perfect light [and] becoming the perfect [light. Whoever has put it on] themselves will go [...] this is the perfect [...] for us to become [...] before we came to [...] whoever receives everything [...] these places, they'll be able to [...] that place, but they'll [... the middle] as incomplete. **77** Only Jesus knows the end of this one.

The holy man is completely holy, down to his (very) body, because if he receives the bread he'll make it holy, or the cup, or anything else that he takes and purifies. Why won't he purify the body too?

As Jesus perfected the water of baptism, that's the way he poured out death. So we go down into the water, but we don't go down into death, so that we won't be poured out into the spirit of the world. When it blows, the winter comes. When the Holy Spirit breathes, the summer comes.

Whoever knows the Truth is a free person, and the free person doesn't sin, because whoever sins is the slave of sin. Truth is the Mother, but knowledge is the joining. Those who aren't given to sin are called free by the world. These who aren't given to sin are made proud by the knowledge of the Truth. That's what makes them free and exalts them over everything. But love builds up, and whoever has been made free through knowledge is a slave because of love for those who aren't yet able to attain [the] freedom of knowledge, [but] knowledge makes them able [to] become free. Love [...] anything its own [...] it [...] its own. It never [says ...] or this is mine, [but ...] are yours. Spiritual love is wine with fragrance. **78** All those who will anoint themselves with it enjoy it. While those who are anointed stay around, those who are nearby also enjoy it. If those who are anointed with ointment leave them and go, those who aren't anointed but are only nearby remain in their stench. The Samaritan didn't give anything to the wounded man except wine with oil. It wasn't anything but the ointment, and it healed the wounds, because love covers a multitude of sins.

The children to whom a woman gives birth will look like the man she loves. If it's her husband, they look like her husband; if it's an adulterer, they look like the adulterer. Often, if a woman sleeps with her husband because she has to, but her heart is with the adulterer with whom she is intimate and she bears a child, the child she bears looks like the adulterer. But you who exist with the Son of God, don't love the world; rather, love the Lord, so that those you'll beget may not come to look like the world, but will come to look like the Lord.

The human unites with the human, the horse unites with the horse, the donkey unites with the donkey. Species unite [with] similar species. That's what it's like when spirit unites with spirit, the [Word] is intimate with the Word, [and light is] intimate [with light. If you] become human, [it's the human who will] love you. If you become [spirit], it's the Spirit who will unite with you. [If] you become word, it's the Word that **79** will unite with you. If [you] become light, it's the light that will be intimate with you. If you become one of those from above, those from above will rest upon you. If you become horse or donkey or calf or dog or sheep or any other of the animals which are outside or below, neither human nor spirit nor Word nor light nor those from above nor those inside will be able to love you. They won't be able to rest within you, and you'll have no part in them.

Whoever is an unwilling slave will be able to be made free. Whoever has become free by the grace of their master and has sold themselves (back) into slavery won't be able to be made free any longer.

CHAP. XIV.

God farms through faith, hope, love, and knowledge. The wise disciple of God will give to each according to the condition of their soul. The son (i.e., priest) of the Son of Humanity (Jesus) can beget (spiritual) children. Undefiled marriage isn't fleshly, but a pure, true mystery.

he world is farmed through four things. They gather into barns through water, earth, wind, and light. And in the same way, God farms through four things too: through faith, hope, love, and knowledge. Our earth is the faith in which we're rooted. [And] the [water] is the hope through which [we're] nourished. The wind is the love through which we grow. And the light [is] the knowledge through which we [ripen.] Grace exists in [four kinds. It's] earthly, it's [heavenly, ...] the heaven of the heaven [...] through [...] Blessed is the one who hasn't

[…] **80** a soul. This one is Jesus Christ. He went all over the place and didn't burden anyone. So, blessed is someone like this; they're a perfect person, because the Word tells us about how hard it is to keep up. How will we be able to achieve such a great thing? How will he give rest to everyone? First and foremost, it's not right to cause anyone grief—whether great or small, or faithless or faithful—and then give rest to those who are (already) at rest among those who are well off. There are some who benefit from giving rest to the one who's well off. Whoever does good can't give rest to them because they can't just do whatever they want; they can't cause grief because they can't cause distress, but sometimes the one who's well off causes them grief. They're not like that, but it's their (own) evil that causes them grief. Whoever has the nature (of the perfect person) gives joy to the one who's good, but some grieve terribly at this.

A householder acquired everything, whether child or slave or cattle or dog or pig or wheat [or] barley or straw or hay or […] or meat and acorn. [But they're] wise and understand what to feed each [one.] To the children they served bread […] but [… the] slaves they served […] and to the cattle [they threw barley] and straw and hay. To [the] dogs they threw bones [and] to [the pigs] they threw acorns **81** and slops. That's what it's like with the disciple of God. If they're wise, they understand what it means to be a disciple. The bodily forms won't deceive them, but they'll look at the condition of the soul of each one and speak with them. There are many animals in the world that are made in human form. (The disciple) recognizes them. To the pigs they'll throw acorns, but to the cattle they'll throw barley with straw and hay. To the dogs they'll throw bones, to the slaves they'll give the appetizer, and to the children they'll give the perfect (food).

There's the Son of Humanity, and there's the son of the Son of Humanity. The Lord is the Son of Humanity, and the son of the Son of Humanity is the one who creates through the Son of Humanity. The Son of Humanity received from God the ability to create. He (also) has the ability to beget. The one who received the ability to create is a creature; the one who received the ability to beget is begotten. The one who creates can't beget; the one who begets can create. They say, The one who creates, begets. But what they beget is a creature. [So] their begotten aren't their children, but they're [...] The one who creates works [publicly,] and are themselves [revealed.] The one who begets, begets [secretly,] and they're hidden [...] the image. [Again,] the one who [creates, creates] publicly, but the one who begets, [begets] children secretly.

No [one will be able to] know [when the husband] **82** and the wife are intimate with each other, except they themselves, because the marriage of the world is a mystery for those who have married. If the defiled marriage is hidden, how much more is the undefiled marriage a true mystery! It's not fleshly, but pure. It isn't of desire, but of the will. It isn't of the darkness or the night, but it's of the day and the light. If a marriage is stripped naked, it becomes pornography—not only if the bride sleeps with another man, but even if she leaves the chamber and is seen, she is unfaithful. Let her reveal herself to her father, her mother, the best man, and the groom's children. They're allowed to enter the bridal chamber every day. But let the others yearn just to hear her voice and enjoy her perfume, and, like dogs, let them eat the crumbs that fall from the table. Grooms and brides belong to the bridal chamber. No one will be able to see the groom and the bride unless [they become] such.

CHAP. XV.

As long as it's hidden, the root of evil is strong, but if it's exposed, it's uprooted. Ignorance is slavery; knowledge is freedom. The mysteries of the Truth are revealed in types and images. The perfect was opened to us with the secrets of the Truth. Those who are separated will unite.

hen Abraham [...] to see what he was going to see, [he] circumcised the flesh of the foreskin, [telling] us that it's necessary to destroy the flesh.

[Most (things)] of [the] world can stand up and live as long as their [insides are hidden. If they're revealed,] they die, as [illustrated] by the visible human. [As long as] the human's guts are hidden, **83** the human is alive. If their guts are exposed and come out of them, the human will die. It's the same way with the tree. While its root is hidden, it blossoms and grows. If its root is exposed, the tree dries up. That's what it's like with everything that's born in the world, not only the revealed, but also the hidden; because as long as the root of evil is hidden, it's strong. But if it's recognized, it dissolves, and if it's revealed, it dies. So the Word says, Already the axe is laid at the root of the trees. It won't (just) cut, (because) that which will be cut blossoms again. Rather, the axe digs down into the ground until it brings up the root. Jesus plucked out the root completely, but others did so partially. As for us, let every one of us dig down to the root of the evil within and pluck it out from its root in us. It'll be uprooted if we recognize it. But if we don't recognize it, it takes root within us and bears its fruit in us. It masters us, and we're forced to serve it. It captures us so that we do what we do [not] want to; and we do [not] do what we want to. [It's] powerful because we haven't recognized it. It's active as long as [it exists.] [Ignorance] is the mother of [all evil.] Ignorance will cause [death, because] what exists from [ignorance] neither did exist nor [does exist,] nor will they come into being [...] **84** they'll be perfected when the whole Truth is revealed, because the Truth is like ignorance. When it's hidden, it rests within itself, but if it's revealed and recognized, it's glorified inasmuch as it's stronger than ignorance and error. It gives freedom. The Word says, If you'll know the Truth, the Truth will make you free. Ignorance is slavery; knowledge is freedom. If we know the Truth, we'll find the fruits of Truth within us. If we unite with it, it'll receive our fullness.

Now we have what's revealed of creation. We say that those who are strong are honorable, but those who are hidden are weak and scorned. That's what it's like with those who are revealed of the Truth; they're weak and scorned, but the hidden are strong and honorable. But the mysteries of the Truth are revealed in types and images.

The chamber is hidden, however; it's the Holy in the Holy. At first, the veil concealed how God managed the creation, but when the veil is torn and what's inside is revealed, then this house will be left behind [like] a desert, or rather, will be [destroyed.] And all divinity will flee [from] these places, not into the Holies [of the] Holies, because it won't be able to unite with the pure [light] and the [flawless] fullness, [but] it'll come to be under the wings of the cross [and under] its arms. This ark will [become their] salvation when the flood **85** of water surges over them. If some belong to the priesthood, they'll be able to enter inside the veil with the high priest. So the veil wasn't torn only at the top, since it would've been open only to those at the top; nor was it torn only at the bottom, since it would've been revealed only to those at the bottom; but it was torn from the top to the bottom. Those at the top opened to us the bottom, so that we'll enter the secret of the Truth. This truly is what's honorable, what's strong, but we'll enter there through scorned types and weaknesses. They're humbled in the presence of the perfect glory. There's glory that's better than glory; there's power that's better than power. So the perfect was opened to us with the secrets of the Truth, and the Holies of the Holies were revealed, and the chamber invited us in.

As long as it's hidden, evil is inactive, but it hasn't been removed from among the Holy Spirit's offspring. They're slaves of evil. But whenever it's revealed, then the perfect light will flow out upon everyone, and all of them who are in it will [receive the chrism.] Then the slaves will be made free and the captives will be redeemed. [Every] plant [which] my Father who's in heaven [hasn't] planted [will be] uprooted. Those who are separated will unite [...] will be filled.

CHAP. XVI.

Conclusion. The mysteries of (divine) marriage are fulfilled in the day and the light. If anyone becomes a child of the bridal chamber, they'll receive the light.

veryone who will [enter] the chamber will kindle their [lamp,] because [it's] like the marriages which are [...] happen at night, the fire [...] **86** at night and is put out. But the mysteries of this marriage are fulfilled in the day and the light. Neither that day nor its light ever sets.

If anyone becomes a child of the bridal chamber, they'll receive the light. If anyone doesn't receive it while they're here, they won't be able to receive it in the other place. Whoever will receive that light won't be seen or bound, and no one will be able to trouble someone like this even while they dwell in the world. Moreover, when they leave the world, they've already received the Truth in the images. The world has become the (eternal) ages, because the (eternal) age is the fullness for them, and it's like this: it's revealed to them alone. It's not hidden in the darkness and the night, but it's hidden in a perfect day and a holy light.

The Gospel According to Philip.

Narrative Gospels

AN UNKNOWN GOSPEL

he main fragments of this Gospel were copied in the second or third century, discovered in 1934, and published in 1935. The two manuscripts that together comprise this text are known as the Egerton Papyrus 2 and the Cologne Papyrus 255. For more information, see Andrew Bernhard, *Other Early Christian Gospels* (T&T Clark, 2007), 84-97.

This Gospel is noteworthy both for its narratives which closely resemble some passages in the New Testament's Gospels, and for a fragmentary miracle story (not otherwise attested) in which Jesus produces fruit on the bank of the Jordan river.

FRAG. I. VERSO.

The Scriptures testify about Jesus. Those who don't believe stand accused by Moses.

o the lawyers [...all] the wrongdoers [...] and not me [...] how does he do it?

[Then he turned] to [the] rulers of the people and made this statement: Search [the] scriptures; [you think] you have life in them. They [testify] about me. Don't [think] I've come to accuse [you] before my Father. [The one who accuses] you is Moses, in whom [you] hope.

But they [said,] We know [well] God [spoke] to Moses, but you—we don't know [where you're from.]

Jesus [said to them] in reply, Now [you] stand accused because [you don't believe those who've been approved] by him; because if [you believed Moses,] you'd believe [me, for] he [wrote] about me to your ancestors [...]

FRAG. I. RECTO.

The crowd cannot seize Jesus. Jesus cures someone who has leprosy.

tones together [so they could stone him.] And the [rulers]

laid their [hands] on him [so that] they might seize him and [deliver him] to the crowd. But they [could] not seize him, because the hour of his arrest [had] not yet [come.] So the Lord escaped [from their hands] and withdrew from [them.]

And look, someone with leprosy approached [him] and said, Teacher Jesus, while I was [traveling] with [others] who had [leprosy] and eating at the inn [with them,] I [contracted leprosy] myself. But if [you want to,] you can cure me.

Now the Lord [said to him, I want to:] be cured. [And immediately] the leprosy left him.

Then Jesus [said to] him, [Go] and show [yourself] to the [priests] and offer [what Moses ordered for] your cure, and don't sin anymore [...]

FRAG. II. RECTO.

Opponents examine Jesus to test him. Jesus quotes Isaiah.

o him, examining him to test him: Teacher Jesus, we know that you've come [from God,] because the things you do [testify] above and beyond all the prophets. [So tell] us: is it right [to give] kings what belongs to them? [Should we pay] them, or [not?]

But since Jesus knew what [they] were thinking, [he scolded them] and asked [them,] Why do you pay me lip service as a Teacher but [don't do] what [I say? Isaiah] accurately prophesied [about] you when he said:

> [These people honor] me with their [lips, but] their [heart] is [far] from [me. They worship me pointlessly ... rules ...]

FRAG. II. VERSO.

Jesus produces fruit on the bank of the Jordan river.

nclosed in the [place ...] being subjected uncertainly [... its] weight unweighed [...] but [while] they were puzzled [as] to [his] strange question, Jesus walked and stood [on the] bank of the Jordan [river.] And reaching out with [his] right hand [...] and he sowed [on] the [...] and then [...] water [...] the [...] and [...] he produced [...] fruit [...]

THE GOSPEL OF PETER

n the second century, a bishop from Antioch found a church using the Gospel of Peter in what is now modern-day Turkey. However, the only known copy today is a Greek fragment discovered in Egypt during the winter of 1886-1887 and first published in 1892. This Greek copy was written sometime between the sixth and ninth centuries. For more information, see my book *The Gospel of Peter: Revisiting Jesus' Death and Resurrection,* published in 2018.

This Gospel is noteworthy for its fantastical portrayal of Jesus' larger-than-life resurrection and for explicitly describing Mary Magdalene as a disciple of Jesus.

CHAP. I.

Herod hands over the Lord to Pilate.

ut of the Jews no one washed their hands, neither Herod nor one of his judges, and when they didn't want to wash, Pilate stood up. And then Herod the king, commanding the Lord to be brought, said to them, Do whatever I commanded you to do to him.

CHAP. II.

Joseph petitions Pilate for the body of the Lord for burial.

nd Joseph stood there, the friend of Pilate and the Lord. And seeing that they were about to crucify him, he went to Pilate and asked for the body of the Lord for burial. And Pilate, having sent to Herod, asked him for the body.

And Herod said, Brother Pilate, even if someone hadn't asked for him, we would've buried him, since also Sabbath is beginning, because it's written in the Law, The sun shouldn't set on one who's been killed.

CHAP. III.

The Lord is tortured and mocked.

nd he handed him over to the people before the first day of their festival of the Unleavened Bread. And those having taken the Lord were running and pushing him. They said, Let's drag the Son of God, having authority over him!

And they were clothing him with purple, and sat him on the seat of judgment. They said, Judge justly, king of Israel! And one of them brought a thorn crown and placed it on the Lord's head.

And other bystanders were spitting in his face, and others slapped his cheeks. Others were piercing him with a reed, and some were scourging him. They said, With this honor, let's honor the Son of God!

CHAP. IV.

The Lord is crucified.

nd they brought two criminals and crucified the Lord in the middle of them, but he was silent, as if having no pain. And when they set up the cross, they wrote: This is the king of Israel. And having laid the clothes in front of him, they divided them and cast lots for them.

But one of those criminals rebuked them. He said, We, because of the wrong that we did, are suffering this way, but this one, having become Savior of humanity—what wrong has he done to you?

And they were angry at him. They commanded that his legs not be broken, so that he might die tortured.

CHAP. V.

The Lord dies. The veil of the temple in Jerusalem is torn in two.

nd it was mid-day, and darkness held fast over all Judea. And they were troubled and distressed that the sun might set, since he was still living. It's written to them, The sun shouldn't set on one who's been killed. And one of them said, Give him bile with sour wine to drink. And having mixed it, they gave it to him to drink. And they fulfilled all things and accumulated the sins on their own heads. And many were going around with

lanterns, thinking it was night, and some fell down.

And the Lord cried out. He said, My Power, the Power, you've left me! And when he said this, it was taken up. And that very hour, the veil of the temple in Jerusalem was torn in two.

CHAP. VI.

The Lord is buried in Joseph's tomb.

nd then they drew the nails from the Lord's hands and placed him on the earth. And the whole earth was shaken, and great fear came.

Then the sun shone and it was found to be the ninth hour. And the Jews rejoiced, and gave his body to Joseph to bury, since he had seen all the good he had done. And having taken the Lord, he washed him and wrapped him in linen, and brought him into his own tomb, which was known as Joseph's Garden.

CHAP. VII.

The elders and priests express remorse. Peter and his companions hide and mourn.

hen the Jews, the elders, and the priests, knowing how much wrong they had done to themselves, began to mourn and say, Woe to our sins. The judgment and the end of Jerusalem is near!

But I and my companions were grieved and hurting inside. We were hiding, because we were being sought by them as criminals and as wanting to burn the temple. On top of all this, we were fasting, sitting, mourning, and weeping night and day until the Sabbath.

CHAP. VIII.

The elders petition Pilate to place guards at the tomb. Pilate assigns Petronius and other soldiers.

nd the scribes, the Pharisees, and the elders gathered together with one another, having heard that all the people were grumbling, beating their chests. They said, If at his death these greatest signs have happened, see how just he was!

The elders were afraid, and went to Pilate, begging him. They said, Give us soldiers, that we may guard his grave

Albrecht Altdorfer, The Resurrection, ca. 1513
Metropolitan Museum of Art

for three days, in case his disciples come and steal him, and the people think that he rose from the dead, and do us wrong.

And Pilate gave them Petronius the centurion, with soldiers to guard the tomb. And elders and scribes went with them to the grave. And having rolled a great stone together with the centurion and the soldiers, all who were there set it at the door of the grave. And they put seven seals on it, and having pitched a tent there, they kept watch.

CHAP. IX.

Two young men descend from heaven, and the stone of the tomb rolls away by itself.

ow when the morning of the Sabbath dawned, a crowd from Jerusalem and the surrounding countryside went to see the grave that had been sealed. But during the night before the Lord's day dawned, while the soldiers were keeping watch two by two, there was a great voice in heaven. And they saw the heavens being opened, and two men descended from there, having much radiance, and they approached the tomb. But that stone which had been placed at the door rolled away by itself, and made way in part, and the tomb was opened, and both the young men went in.

CHAP. X.

Three men come out of the tomb, followed by a cross.

hen the soldiers who had seen this woke up the centurion and the elders, because they were there too, keeping guard. And while they were explaining to them what they saw, again they saw three men coming out of the tomb, with the two supporting the one, and a cross following them. And the heads of the two reached as far as heaven, but that of the one being led by them reached beyond the heavens.

And they heard a voice from the heavens ask, Have you proclaimed to those who sleep?

And a response was heard from the cross: Yes!

CHAP. XI.

The soldiers hurry back to Pilate and describe all that they saw.

hen those men decided to go with each other and report these things to Pilate. And while they were still deliberating, again the heavens were seen being opened, and a certain man descended and went into the grave.

Having seen these things, those with the centurion hurried by night to Pilate, having left the tomb they were watching. Greatly distressed, they described everything they saw and said, Truly he was the Son of God!

In response Pilate said, I'm clean of the blood of the Son of God, and this is clear to us.

Then all who came were begging him and encouraging him to command the centurion and the soldiers to say nothing about what they saw.

They said, It's better for us to be guilty of a great sin in front of God than to fall into the hands of the Jewish people and be stoned.

So Pilate commanded the centurion and the soldiers to say nothing.

CHAP. XII.

Mary Magdalene and her friends go to the tomb.

ow at dawn on the Lord's day, Mary Magdalene, a disciple of the Lord, afraid because of the Jews (since they were inflamed by anger), had not done at the Lord's grave what women usually do for their loved ones who've died.

Taking her friends with her, she went to the grave where he was laid. And they were afraid that the Jews might see them.

They said, If on the day he was crucified we weren't able to weep and mourn, even now we might do this on his grave. But who will roll away for us the stone that has been placed at the door of the grave so that we might go in, sit by him, and do our duties? Because the stone is great, and we're afraid that someone might see us. And if we aren't able, at least let's place at the door what we're bringing in memory of him, and we'll weep and mourn until we return to our house.

CHAP. XIII.

The women encounter a certain young man sitting in the tomb.

nd having gone, they found that the tomb had been opened.

And having approached, they bent down and saw there a certain young man sitting in the middle of the tomb. He was beautiful, having clothed himself with a long, shining robe. He asked them, Why did you come? Whom do you seek? Not that one who was crucified? He arose and went away. But if you don't believe, bend down and see where he was lying, that he's not there, because he arose and went to where he came from.

Then the women were afraid, and fled.

CHAP. XIV.

The twelve disciples return to their houses. Simon Peter, Andrew, and Levi take their nets and go to the sea.

Now it was the last day of the Unleavened Bread, and many people were leaving, returning to their houses, the festival being over. But we, the twelve disciples of the Lord, were weeping and grieving, and each of us grieving because of what had happened, returned home. But I, Simon Peter, and my brother Andrew, having taken our nets, went off to the sea. And with us was Levi, the son of Alphaeus, whom the Lord [...]

Mystical
Gospels
Cum Priuilegio.

THE SECRET BOOK OF JAMES

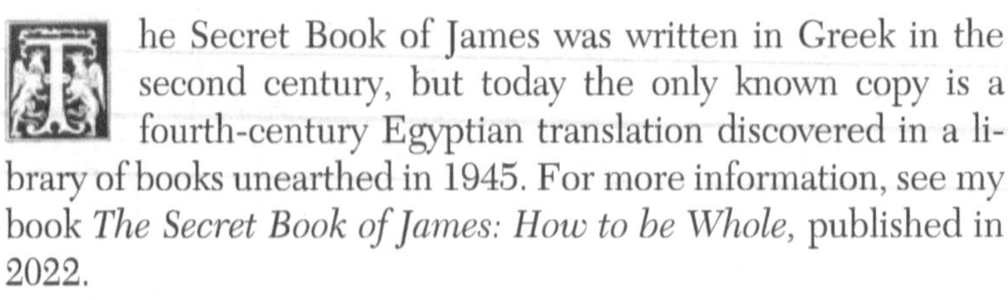

The Secret Book of James was written in Greek in the second century, but today the only known copy is a fourth-century Egyptian translation discovered in a library of books unearthed in 1945. For more information, see my book *The Secret Book of James: How to be Whole,* published in 2022.

This text is noteworthy for including early parables attributed to Jesus. Interestingly, the author seems unaware of the story of the empty tomb from the Gospels, as Jesus is described as being "buried in the sand." Historically, that's what the Romans typically did to those they crucified—dumped the bodies into shallow graves.

As an esoteric text, this book is intentionally opaque, inviting readers to ponder its meanings and paradoxes.

CHAP. I.

James writes a secret book about what the Savior revealed.

James writes] to […]: Peace [to you from] peace, [love from] love, [grace] from grace, [faith] from faith, life from holy life!

Since you asked me to send you a secret book revealed to Peter and me by the Lord, and I could neither turn you down nor talk to you (directly), [I've written] it in Hebrew letters and have sent it to you—and to you alone. But as a minister of the salvation of the saints, take care not to tell too many people about this book, which the Savior didn't want to tell all twelve of us, the disciples. But blessed are those who will be saved through the faith of this message.

Ten months ago, I sent you another secret book that the Savior revealed to me. But think of that one as revealed **2** to me, James. And this one […]

Albrecht Altdorfer, The Ascension of Christ, ca. 1513
Metropolitan Museum of Art

CHAP. II.

The twelve disciples are writing their books about what the Savior had told them. The Savior appears and takes James and Peter aside.

ow all twelve disciples [were] sitting together [at the same time] recalling what the Savior had told each of them, whether privately or publicly, and organizing it in books. [But I] was writing what went into [my book.] Look! The Savior appeared, [after] he had left [us, while we were watching] for him. Five hundred and fifty days after he had risen from the dead, we told him, You went away and left us!

But Jesus said, No, but I'll return to the place from which I came. If you want to come with me, come on!

In response they all said, We'll come if you tell us to.

He said, Truly I tell you, no one will ever enter the kingdom of heaven because I ordered it, but because you yourselves are full. Leave James and Peter to me so that I may fill them.

After he called these two, he took them aside and told the rest to keep doing what they were doing.

CHAP. III.

The Savior calls James and Peter to sobriety. He exhorts them to be full of the Spirit.

he Savior said, You've received mercy. **3** [...] they [haven't] understood. Don't you want to be filled? Your hearts are drunk. Don't you, then, want to be sober? Then be ashamed! From now on, awake or asleep, remember that you've seen the Son of Humanity, and have talked to him in person, and have heard him in person.

Woe to those who've seen the Son of Humanity! Blessed are those who haven't seen that man, mingled with him, spoken to him, or heard a thing he's said. Yours is life! Know, then, that he healed you when you were sick, so that you might reign.

Woe to those who've found relief from their sickness, because they'll relapse into sickness. Blessed are those who haven't been sick and have found relief before getting sick. Yours is the kingdom of God! So I tell you, be full and leave no space within you empty, because the one who is coming will be able to mock you.

Then Peter replied, Three times you've told us **4** to be [full, but] we are full.

In [response the Savior] said, That's why I [told] you [be full]—so that you won't [be lacking. Those who are lacking] won't [be saved.] It's good to be full [and] bad [to be lacking.] So just as it's good for you to be lacking and bad for you to be full, whoever is full is also lacking. One who's lacking isn't filled the same way that someone who's lacking is filled, and anyone who's full gets everything they need. So it's right to be lacking while it's possible to fill you, and to be filled while it's possible to be lacking, so that you can [fill] yourselves more. So [be] full of the Spirit but lacking in reason, because reason is of the soul—in fact, it is soul.

CHAP. IV.

The Lord exhorts James and Peter to stop loving the flesh and being afraid of sufferings. The kingdom of God belongs to those who have believed in his cross.

n response I told him, Lord, we can obey you if you want us to, because we've abandoned our fathers, our mothers, and our villages, and have followed you. So help us not to be tempted by the devil, the evil one.

In response the Lord asked, What good is it to you if you do the will of the Father, and he doesn't give it to you as a gift when you're tempted by Satan? But if you're oppressed by Satan and persecuted and do (God's) **5** will, I [say] that (God) will love you, make you my equal, and regard [you] as having become beloved through his forethought by your own choice. So won't you stop loving the flesh and being afraid of sufferings? Or don't you know that you haven't yet been abused, unjustly accused, locked up in prison, illegally condemned, crucified by (human) reason, nor buried in the sand as I myself was by the evil one? Do you dare to spare the flesh, you for whom the Spirit is a surrounding wall? If you consider how long the world existed <before> you, and how long it will exist after you, you'll find that your life is a single day and your sufferings a single hour. For the good won't come into the world. So scorn death and take thought for life! Remember my cross and my death, and you'll live!

But in response I told him, Lord, don't teach us about the cross and death, because they're far **6** from you.

In response the Lord said, Truly I tell you, no one will be saved unless they [believe] in my cross, [because] the kingdom of God belongs to those who've believed in my cross. So become those who seek death, like the dead who seek life; because what they seek is revealed to them. So what do they have to worry about? When you turn to the subject of death, it will teach you about election. Truly I tell you, no one who's afraid of death will be saved, because the kingdom of <God> belongs to those who are put to death. Become better than I; be like the child of the Holy Spirit.

CHAP. V.

The Lord explains how the head of prophecy was cut off with John. He no longer speaks in parables. He teaches about the kingdom of God.

hen I asked him, Lord, how can we prophesy to those who ask us to prophesy to them? Because there are many who ask us, and who look to us to hear a message from us.

In response the Lord asked, Don't you know that the head of prophecy was cut off with John?

But I asked, Lord, is it possible to remove the head of prophecy?

The Lord told me, When you realize what the head means, and that prophecy comes from the head, understand what it means that its head was removed. **7** At first I spoke to you in parables, and you didn't understand. Now I speak to you openly, and you still don't perceive. But to me you were a parable of parables and something visible out in the open.

Be eager to be saved without being urged. Rather, be ready on your own and, if possible, get there before me, because the Father will love you.

Come to hate hypocrisy and evil intention, because intention is what produces hypocrisy, and hypocrisy is far from the Truth.

Don't let the kingdom of heaven wither, because it's

like a date palm shoot whose fruit has poured down around it. It sent out some leaves, and after they sprouted, they made their productivity dry up. This is also what happened with the fruit that came from this single root; when it was picked, many acquired fruit. Wouldn't it truly be good if you could produce the new plants now? <You> would find it.

Since I've already been glorified like this, why do you hold me back in my eagerness to go? **8** For after the [labor,] you've made me stay with you another eighteen days because of the parables. For some people, it was enough <to listen> to the teaching and understand The Shepherds, The Seed, The Building, The Lamps of the Young Women, The Wage of the Workers, and The Silver Coins and the Woman.

Be eager about the message! The first stage of the message is faith, the second is love, and the third is works, because from these comes life.

The message is like a grain of wheat. When someone sowed it, they believed in it, and when it sprouted, they loved it, because they saw many grains in place of one. And after they worked, they were saved because they prepared it as food, then kept enough left over to be sown. This is also how you yourselves can receive the kingdom of heaven. Unless you receive it through knowledge, you won't be able to find it.

CHAP. VI.

The Lord exhorts James and Peter to be saved and to follow him. He urges them to pray to God often.

So I tell you, be sober! Don't be deceived. And many times I told you all together—and also to you alone, James, I've said—Be saved! And I've commanded you to follow me, and I've taught you what to do in the face of the rulers.

See that I've come down, spoken, been torn, and taken my crown **9** when I saved you, because I came down to dwell with you so that you'll dwell with me. And when I found your houses without ceilings, I lived in the houses that could receive me at the time I came down.

Trust me about this, my brothers (i.e., Peter and James). Understand what the great light is. The Father doesn't need me, because a father doesn't need a son, but it's the son who needs the father. I'm going to him, because the Father of the Son doesn't need you.

Listen to the message, understand knowledge, love life, and no one will persecute or oppress you other than you yourselves.

You wretches! You poor devils! You hypocrites of the Truth! You falsifiers of knowledge! You sinners against the Spirit! Can you still bear to listen, when you should've been speaking from the beginning? Can you still bear to sleep, when you should've been awake from the beginning so that the kingdom of heaven might receive you?

10 Truly I tell you, it's easier for a holy person to fall into defilement, and for an enlightened person to fall into darkness, than for you to reign—or not reign.

I've remembered your tears, your grief, and your pain. They're far from us. But now, you who are outside of the Father's inheritance, weep where it's necessary, grieve, and proclaim what's good as the Son is ascending as he should.

Truly I tell you, if I had been sent (only) to those who would listen to me and had spoken to them (alone), I wouldn't ever have gone up from the earth. Now, then, be ashamed for these things!

Look, I'll leave you and go away. I don't want to continue with you anymore, just as you yourselves don't want that. Now, then, follow me eagerly. That's why I tell you that I came down for you. You're beloved; you'll bring life for many. Call on the Father. Pray to God often, and he will be generous with you.

Blessed is the one who has seen you with (God) when (God) was proclaimed among the angels and given glory among the holy ones; yours is life. Rejoice and be glad as **11** children of God. Keep his will so that you may be saved. Accept my warning and save yourselves. I'm pleading for you with the Father, who will forgive you much.

CHAP. VII.

The Lord pronounces woes and teaches about the flesh, the body, the soul, and the spirit.

nd when we heard these things, we were delighted, because we had been depressed about the things we mentioned before.

But when he saw us rejoicing, he said, Woe to you who need an advocate! Woe to you who need grace! Blessed will be those who've spoken out and acquired grace for themselves!

Be like foreigners. How are they viewed in your city? Why are you disturbed when you cast yourselves out on your own and separate yourselves from your city? Why do you leave your dwelling on your own and make it available for those who want to live in it? You outcasts and runaways! Woe to you, because you'll be caught!

Or do you think that the Father is a lover of humanity, or is persuaded by prayers, or grants grace to one on behalf of another, or puts up with one who seeks?

(God) knows about desire and what the flesh needs. It's not this (flesh) which desires the soul, because without the soul, the body doesn't sin, just as **12** the soul isn't saved without the spirit. But if the soul is saved without evil, and the spirit is also saved, then the body becomes sinless. For it's the spirit that raises the soul, but the body that kills it; that is, (the soul) kills itself.

Truly I tell you, (God) won't ever forgive the sin of the soul or the guilt of the flesh, because no one who's worn the flesh will be saved. Do you think that many have found the kingdom of heaven? Blessed is the one who's seen oneself (at) the fourth (stage) in heaven.

CHAP. VIII.

The Lord comforts the disciples and teaches about the kingdom of God.

hen we heard these things, we felt depressed. But when he saw that we were depressed, he said, I'm telling you this so that you may know yourselves. For the kingdom of heaven is like an ear of grain after it had sprouted in a field. And when it had ripened, it scattered its fruit, and again it filled the field with ears of grain for another year. You, too, be eager to reap an ear of the grain of life for yourselves so that you may be filled with the kingdom!

And as long as I'm with you, pay attention to me and trust

in me, but when I leave you, remember me. And remember me because when I was with you, you didn't know me. Blessed are those who've known me. Woe to those who've heard and haven't believed! Blessed will be those who **13** haven't seen, [but ...]!

And once again I [appeal to] you, because I'm revealed to you building a house very valuable to you when you take shelter under it, just as it will be able to support your neighbors' house when it threatens to fall. Truly I tell you, woe to those for whom I was sent down to this place! Blessed will be those who go up to the Father. Again I warn you, you who are. Be like those who are not so that you may be with those who are not.

Don't let the kingdom of heaven become a desert within you. Don't be haughty because of the light that enlightens, but behave toward yourselves the way that I've behaved toward you. I've put myself under the curse for you, so that you may be saved.

CHAP. IX.

The Lord shares his final words and is taken up in a chariot of the Spirit.

ut in response to these comments Peter said, Sometimes you urge us on to the kingdom of heaven, and again at other times you turn us away, Lord. Sometimes you persuade and draw us to faith and promise us life, and again at other times you cast us out of the kingdom of heaven.

But in response the Lord told us, I've given you faith many times. Moreover, I've revealed myself to you, **14** James, and you haven't known me. Now again, I see you rejoicing often. And when you're delighted about the promise of life, nevertheless you're sad and depressed when you're taught about the kingdom.

But through faith and knowledge, you've received life. Despise rejection when you hear it, but when you hear the promise, rejoice all the more. Truly I tell you, whoever will receive life and believe the kingdom will never leave it—not even if the Father wants to banish them!

This is all I'm going to tell you up to this point, but now I'll go up to the place from which I came. But when I was eager to go, you cast me out, and instead of accompanying me, you've chased me away.

But be attentive to the glory that awaits me, and when you've opened your hearts, listen to the hymns that await me up in heaven, because today I need to sit at the right hand of the Father.

Now I've spoken (my) last word to you, and I'll leave you, because a chariot of the Spirit has taken me up, and from now on I'll strip myself so that I may clothe myself. But pay attention: Blessed are those who've proclaimed the Son before his coming down so that when I've come, I might go up. Blessed three **15** times over are those who [were] proclaimed by the Son before they came to be, so that you may have a portion with them.

CHAP. X.

James and Peter ascend to heaven as Jesus did.

hen he said these things, he left. But Peter and I knelt down, gave thanks, and sent our hearts up to heaven. We heard with our ears, and saw with our eyes, the cacophony of wars and a trumpet blare and a great commotion.

And when we passed beyond that place, we sent our minds up higher and heard with our ears hymns and angelic praises and angelic rejoicing. And heavenly majesties were singing hymns, and we rejoiced too.

After this again, we wanted to send our spirit up to the Majesty. And after we went up, we weren't allowed to see or hear anything, because the other disciples called us and asked us, What did you hear from the Teacher? and, What did he tell you? and, Where did he go?

But in response we told them, He went up. And he's given us his right hand and promised us all life, and he revealed to us children who are to come after us, after telling **16** [us] to love them, as we'd be [saved] because of them.

CHAP. XI.

James' concluding words.

nd when they heard, they believed the revelation indeed, but were angry about those to be born. So, not wanting to give them a scandal, I sent each of them to a different place. But I myself went up to Jerusalem, praying to acquire a portion with the beloved ones who will be revealed.

And I pray that the beginning may come from you, because this is how I can be saved, since they'll be enlightened through me, by my faith—and through another (faith) that's even better than mine, because I want mine to be the lesser.

So do your best to be like them, and pray that you acquire a portion with them. Apart from what I've said, the Savior didn't disclose a revelation for them. We do indeed proclaim a portion with those for whom the proclamation was made—those whom the Lord has (accepted as) children.

THE GOSPEL OF TRUTH

he Gospel of Truth was written in Greek in the second century, but the only known copies today are two fourth-century Egyptian translations that were discovered in 1945. For more information, see my book *The Gospel of Truth: The Mystical Gospel,* published in 2018.

The Gospel of Truth is not a Gospel in the traditional sense, but rather a homily urging unity in the Church. One noteworthy feature is its highly symbolic language, which operates on multiple levels simultaneously.

Though complex in its imagery and deeply layered poetic rhetoric, the Gospel of Truth is simple in its core message: All come from God and will ultimately return to God. Ignorance and Error distract us with frightening illusions, but when we disregard Error and turn to God, we come to the spiritual rest of completion, like plants flourishing in God's paradise.

CHAP. I.

The Gospel of Truth is a joy.

he Gospel of Truth is a joy for those who've received grace from the Father of Truth, that they might know him through the power of the Word that came from the fullness—the one who's in the thought and mind of the Father. They call him Savior. That's the name of the work he'll do to redeem those who had become **17** ignorant of the Father. And the word Gospel is the revelation of hope, the discovery of those who search for him.

CHAP. II.

Disregard Error, since it has no root. The forgetfulness of Error didn't come into being from the Father.

ince all searched for the one from whom they had come—all were within him, the uncontainable, inconceivable one who's beyond every thought

—(and) since ignorance of the Father caused anguish and terror, and the anguish grew thick like a fog, so that no one could see—Error was strengthened. It worked on its own matter in vain, not knowing the Truth.

It happened in a deluding way, as (Error) prepared with power, in beauty, a substitute for the Truth. Now this wasn't humiliating for the uncontainable, inconceivable one, because the anguish and forgetfulness and delusion of deceit were like nothing, whereas the Truth is established, unchangeable, unperturbed, beyond beauty. Because of this, disregard Error, since it has no root.

It happened in a fog concerning the Father. It happens (now) since (Error) prepares works in forgetfulness and terror, so that with them (Error) might attract those in the middle and imprison them.

The forgetfulness of Error wasn't revealed; it wasn't a **18** [thought] from the Father. Forgetfulness didn't come into being from the Father, though it did come into being because of him. What comes into being within him is the knowledge, which was revealed so that forgetfulness might be dissolved, and the Father might be known. Forgetfulness came into being because the Father was unknown, so when the Father comes to be known, forgetfulness won't exist anymore.

CHAP. III.

Through the Gospel, Jesus Christ enlightened those who were in darkness through forgetfulness. As a result, Error was angry. They nailed Jesus to a tree, and he became the fruit of the Father's knowledge. All need the Father. Jesus took the Book of the Living. He put on that book, was nailed to a tree, and published the Father's edict on the cross.

his is the Gospel of the one they search for, revealed to those who are complete through the mercies of the Father, the hidden mystery. Through (the Gospel,) Jesus Christ enlightened those who were in darkness through forgetfulness. He enlightened them; he showed them a Way, and the Way is the Truth which he taught them.

As a result, Error was angry. It pursued him. It was threatened by him and brought to nothing. They nailed (Jesus) to a tree, and he became the fruit of the Father's knowledge. However, (the fruit) didn't cause destruction when it was eaten, but those who ate it were given joy in the discovery. He discovered them in himself and they discovered him in themselves.

As for the uncontainable, inconceivable one—the Father, the complete one who made all—all are within him, and all need him. Although he kept their completion within himself which he didn't give to all, the Father wasn't jealous. Indeed, what jealousy is there between him and his members? **19** For if, like this, the generation [received the completion,] they couldn't have come […] the Father. He keeps their completion within himself, giving it to them to return to him with a unitary knowledge in completion. He's the one who made all, and all are within him, and all need him.

Like someone who's unknown, he wants to be known and loved—because what did all need if not the knowledge of the Father?

He became a guide, peaceful and leisurely. He came and spoke the Word as a teacher in places of learning. Those who were wise in their own estimation came up to him to test him, but he confounded them because they were vain. They hated him because they weren't wise in Truth. After all of them, all the little children came too; theirs is the knowledge of the Father. When they were strengthened, they received teaching about the Father's expressions. They knew and they were known; they received glory and they gave glory. In their hearts the living Book of the Living was revealed, which was written in the thought and mind **20** [of the] Father, and before the [foundation] of all within his incomprehensibility. This (book) is impossible to take, since it permits the one who takes it to be killed. No one could've been revealed among those who'd been entrusted with salvation unless the book had appeared. Because of this, the merciful and faithful Jesus patiently suffered until he took that book, since he knows that his death is life for many.

When a will hasn't yet been opened, the wealth of the deceased master of the house is hidden; so too all were hidden while the Father of all was invisible. They were from him,

Albrecht Altdorfer, The Raising of the Cross, ca. 1513
National Gallery of Art

from whom every realm comes. Because of this, Jesus was revealed, put on that book, was nailed to a tree, and published the Father's edict on the cross. Oh, what a great teaching! Drawing himself down to death, he clothed himself in eternal life, stripped himself of the perishable rags, and clothed himself in incorruptibility, which no one can take from him.

When he entered the empty realms of terror, he passed through those who were stripped by forgetfulness, being knowledge and completion, proclaiming the things that are in the heart **21** [...] teach those who will [receive teaching.]

CHAP. IV.

Those who will receive teaching are the living who are written in the Book of the Living. It's necessary for all to go up to the Father. If someone has knowledge, they're from above. The letters of the living book are letters of Truth.

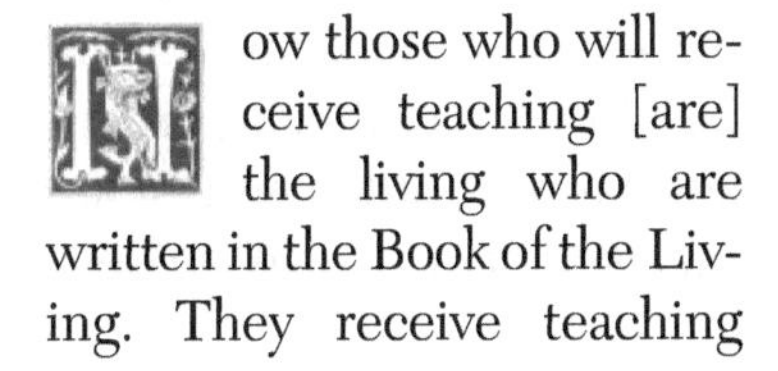

ow those who will receive teaching [are] the living who are written in the Book of the Living. They receive teaching about themselves, and they receive it from the Father, returning to him again.

Since the completion of all is in the Father, it's necessary for all to go up to him. Then, if someone has knowledge, they receive what are their own, and he draws them to himself, because the one who's ignorant is in need. And it's a great need, since they need what will complete them. Since the completion of all is in the Father, it's necessary for all to go up to him, and for each one to receive what are their own. He inscribed these things beforehand, having prepared them to give to those who came out from him.

Those whose names he knew beforehand were called at the end, so that the one who has knowledge is the one whose name the Father has called, because those whose name hasn't been spoken are ignorant. Indeed, how can someone hear if their name hasn't been called? For the one who's ignorant until the end is a delusion of forgetfulness, and they'll dissolve with it. Otherwise, why do these miserable ones have no **22** name? Why do they have no voice?

So if someone has knowledge, they're from above. If they're called, they hear, they reply, and they turn to the one who calls them. And they go up to him, and they know how they are called. Having knowledge, they do the will of the one who called them, they want to please him, and they receive rest. Each one's name becomes their own. The one who has knowledge like this knows where they come from and where they're going. They know like one who, having been drunk, turns from their drunkenness, and having returned to themselves, restores what are their own.

He's returned many from Error. He went before them to the realms from which they had moved away. They had received Error because of the depth of the one who surrounds every realm, though nothing surrounds him. It's a great wonder that they were in the Father, not knowing him, and that they were able to come out by themselves, since they weren't able to grasp and know the one in whom they were. He revealed his will as knowledge in harmony with all that emanated from him.

This is the knowledge of the living book which he revealed to the **23** generations at the end, letters from him revealing how they're not vowels or consonants, so that one might read them and think they're meaningless, but they're letters of the Truth—they speak and know themselves. Each letter is a complete thought, like a book that's complete, since they're letters written by the Unity, the Father having written them so that the generations, by means of his letters, might know the Father.

CHAP. V.

The Word of the Father goes out in all. The Father reveals his bosom, and his bosom is the Holy Spirit. He reveals what's hidden of himself, his Son. Knowledge dissolves ignorance. In time, Unity will complete the realms.

is Wisdom meditates on the Word, his teaching speaks it, his knowledge has revealed it, his patience is a crown upon it, his joy is in harmony with it, his glory has exalted it, his image has revealed it, his rest has received it, his love made a body around it, his faith embraced it.

In this way, the Word of the Father goes out in all, as the fruit **24** [of] his heart and an expression of his will. But it supports all. It chooses them and also takes the expression of all, purifying them, returning them to the Father and to the Mother, Jesus of infinite sweetness.

The Father reveals his bosom, and his bosom is the Holy Spirit. He reveals what's hidden of himself; what's hidden of himself is his Son—so that through the mercies of the Father, the generations may know him and cease their work in searching for the Father, resting in him and knowing that this is the rest. He's filled the need and dissolved its appearance—its appearance is the world in which it served, because where there's envy and strife there's need, but where there's Unity there's completion. Since need came into being because the Father wasn't known, when the Father is known, from then on, need will no longer exist. As someone's ignorance dissolves when they gain knowledge, and as darkness dissolves when the light appears, **25** so also need dissolves in completion. So the appearance is revealed from then on, but it'll dissolve in the harmony of Unity.

For now, their works lie scattered. In time, Unity will complete the realms. Within Unity each one will receive themselves, and within knowledge they'll purify themselves from multiplicity into Unity, consuming matter within themselves like fire, and darkness by light, death by life. If indeed these things have happened to each one of us, then it's right for us to think about all, so that this house will be holy and silent for the Unity.

CHAP. VI.

The Parable of the Jars.

It's like some who've left their home, having jars that weren't any good in places. They broke them, but the master of the house doesn't suffer any loss. Instead he rejoices, because in place of the bad jars are ones that are full and complete. For this is **26** the judgment that's come from above; it's judged everyone. It's a drawn, two-edged sword which cuts both ways. The Word, which is in the hearts of those who speak it, appeared. It isn't just a sound, but it was incarnated (embodied).

A great disturbance arose among the jars, because some were empty, others filled; some provided for, others poured out; some purified, others broken. All the realms were shaken and disturbed, because they didn't have order or stability. Error was anxious. It didn't know what to do; it grieved, mourned, and hurt itself, because it knew nothing. The knowledge, which is (Error's) destruction, approached (Error) and all that emanated from it. Error is empty, with nothing inside it.

Truth came into their midst, and all that emanated knew it. They welcomed the Father in Truth with a complete power that joins them with the Father. Truth is the Father's mouth; the Holy Spirit is his tongue. Everyone who loves the Truth and are joined to the **27** Truth are joined to the Father's mouth. By his tongue they'll receive the Holy Spirit. This is the revelation of the Father and his manifestation to his generations. He revealed what was hidden of himself; he explained it, because who has anything, if not the Father alone?

CHAP. VII.

Every realm emanates from the Father. Those who didn't exist at all won't exist.

very realm emanates from him. They know they've come out from him like children who are from someone who's completely mature. They knew they hadn't yet received form or a name. The Father gives birth to each one. Then, when they receive form from his knowledge, although they're really within him, they don't know him. But the Father is complete, knowing every realm that's within him. If he wants to, he reveals whomever he wants, giving them a form and a name. He gives a name to them, and causes those to come into being who, before they come into being, are ignorant of the one who made them.

I'm not saying, then, that those who haven't yet come into being are nothing, but they exist **28** in the one who will want them to come into being when he wants, like a later time. Before everything is revealed, he knows what he'll produce. But the fruit which he hasn't yet revealed doesn't yet know anything, nor does it do anything. In addition, every realm which is itself in the Father is from the one who exists, who establishes them from what doesn't exist. For those who have no root have no fruit either. They think to themselves, I've come into being, but they'll dissolve by themselves. Because of this, those who didn't exist at all won't exist.

CHAP. VIII.

The Parable of Nightmares.

hat, then, did he want them to think of themselves?

He wanted to them to think, I've come into being like the shadows and phantoms of the night. When the light shines on the terror which they received, they know that it's nothing. In this way, they were ignorant of the Father, whom **29** they didn't see. Since it was terror and disturbance and instability and doubt and division, many illusions were at work among them, and vain ignorance, like they were deep in sleep and found themselves in nightmares. Either they're running somewhere, or unable to run away from someone; or they're fighting, or being beaten; or they've fallen from heights, or fly through the air without wings. Sometimes, too, it's like someone is killing them, even though no one's chasing them; or they themselves are killing those around them, covered in their blood. Until those who are going through all these nightmares can wake up, they see nothing, because these things are nothing.

That's the way it is with those who've cast off ignorance like sleep. They don't regard it as anything, nor do they regard its **30** other works as real, but they abandon them like a dream in the night. They value the knowledge of the Father like they value the light. The ignorant have acted like they're asleep; those who've come to knowledge have acted like they've awakened. Good for the one who returns and awakens! Blessed is the one who's opened the eyes of those who can't see! The Holy Spirit hurried after them to revive them. Having given a hand to the one who lay on the ground, it set them up on their feet, because they hadn't yet arisen. It gave them the knowledge of the Father and the revelation of the Son, because when they saw him and heard him, he granted them to taste him and to grasp the beloved Son.

CHAP. IX.

When the Son was revealed, he taught about the Father. He became a Way for those who were led astray.

hen he was revealed, he taught them about the Father, the uncontainable one, and breathed into them what's in the thought, doing his will. When many had received the light, they turned **31** to him. For the material ones were strangers, who didn't see his form or know him. For he came by means of fleshly form, and nothing could block his path, because incorruptibility can't be grasped. Moreover, he said new things while he spoke about what's in the Father's heart and brought out the complete Word. When the light spoke through his mouth, and by his voice gave birth to life, he gave them thought, wisdom, mercy, salvation, and the Spirit of power from the infinity and sweetness of the Father. He caused punishments and torments to cease, because they led astray into Error and bondage those who needed mercy. He dissolved and confounded them with knowledge. He became a Way for those who were led astray, knowledge for those who were ignorant, a discovery for those who were searching, strength for those who were wavering, and purity for those who were impure.

CHAP. X.

The Parable of the Sheep.

e's the shepherd who left behind the ninety- **32** nine sheep which weren't lost. He went and searched for the one which was lost. He rejoiced when he found it, because ninety-nine is a number expressed with the left hand. However, when the one is found, the numerical sum moves to the right hand. In this way, what needs the one—that is, the whole right hand—draws what it needs, takes it from the left hand, and moves it to the right, so the number becomes one hundred. This is a symbol of the sound of these numbers; this is the Father.

Even on the Sabbath, he worked for the sheep which he found fallen in the pit. He saved the life of the sheep, having brought it up from the pit, so that you may know in your hearts—you're children of the knowledge of the heart—what is the Sabbath, on which it isn't right for salvation to be idle, so that you may speak of the day which is above, which has no night, and of the light that doesn't set, because it's complete. Speak then from the heart, because you're the completed day, and the light that doesn't cease dwells within you. Speak of the Truth with those who search for it, and of knowledge with those who've sinned in their Error. **33**

CHAP. XI.

Help those who stumble, reach out to those who are sick, feed those who are hungry, and give rest to those who are weary. Be concerned about yourselves. Don't be concerned about other things. Do the Father's will.

trengthen the feet of those who stumble, and reach out to those who are sick. Feed those who are hungry, and give rest to those who are weary. Raise up those who want to arise, and awaken those who sleep, because you're the understanding that's unsheathed. If strength is like this, it becomes stronger.

Be concerned about yourselves. Don't be concerned about other things which you've rejected from yourselves. Don't return to eat your vomit. Don't be eaten by worms, because you've already shaken it off. Don't become a dwelling-place for the devil, because you've already brought him to naught. Don't strengthen your obstacles which are collapsing, as though you're a support. For the lawless one is nothing, to be treated more harshly than the just, doing his works among others.

Do then the Father's will, because you're from him. For the Father is sweet, and goodness is in his will. He knows what's yours, that you may find rest in them. For by the fruits they know what's yours, because the children of the Father **34** are his fragrance, since they're from the grace of his expression. Because of this, the Father loves his fragrance, and reveals it in every place. And when it mixes with matter, it gives his fragrance to the light, and in tranquility he causes it to rise above every form and every sound. For it's not the ears that smell the fragrance, but it's the Spirit that smells, and draws the fragrance to itself, and sinks down into the Father's fragrance. He shelters it, then, and takes it to the place from which it came, from the first fragrance which has grown cold. It's something in a soul-endowed delusion, like cold water sunk into loose earth. Those who see it think that it's just earth. Afterwards, it dissolves again. If a breath draws it, it becomes warm. So the fragrances which are cold are from the division. Because of this, faith came. It dissolved the division, and it brought the fullness that's warm with love, so that the cold may not return, but rather the unitary thought of completion.

CHAP. XII.

Return to the Father is called repentance. The doctor hurries to the place where there's sickness. Those who return will be anointed with ointment, which is the Father's mercy.

his is the Word of the Gospel of the discovery of the fullness, which comes for those who are awaiting **35** the salvation which is coming from above. The hope for which they're waiting is waiting for those whose image is light with no shadow in it. If at that time the fullness comes, the need of matter doesn't come through the infinity of the Father, who comes to give time to the need—although no one can say that the incorruptible one will come like this. But the depth of the Father multiplied, and the thought of Error didn't exist with him. It's something that's fallen, which is easily set upright in the discovery of the one who's to come to what he'll return, because the return is called repentance.

Because of this, incurruptibility breathed out. It followed after the one who sinned, so that they might rest, because forgiveness is what remains for the light in need, the Word of fullness. For the doctor hurries to the place where there's sickness, because that's what he (or she) wants to do. The one in need, then, doesn't hide it, because (the doctor) has what they need. In this way the fullness, which has no need but fills the need, is what he **36** provided from himself to fill up what's needed, so that they might receive grace; because when they were in need, they didn't have grace. Because of this, a diminishing took place where there is no grace. When what was diminished was restored, what they needed was revealed as fullness. This is the discovery of the light of Truth which enlightened them, because it doesn't change.

Because of this, they spoke of Christ in their midst: Seek, and those who were disturbed will receive a return—and he'll anoint them with ointment. The ointment is the mercy of the Father, who will have mercy on them. But those whom he anointed are those who have been completed, because full jars are the ones that are anointed. But when the anointing of one dissolves, it empties, and the cause of the need is the place where the ointment leaks, because a breath and its power draws it. But from the one who has no need, no seal is removed, nor is anything emptied, but what it needs is filled again by the Father, who's complete.

CHAP. XIII.

The Father's paradise is a place of rest. The Word was the first to come out from the Father. Nothing happens without the will of the Father.

e's good. He knows his plants, because he planted them in his paradise. Now his paradise is a place of rest. This **37** is the completion in the Father's thought, and these are the words of his meditation. Each of his words is the work of his one will in the revelation of his Word. When they were still in the depths of his thought, the Word—which was the first to come out—revealed them along with a mind that speaks the one Word in a silent grace. He was called the Thought, since they were in it before being revealed. It happened, then, that he was the first to come out at the time when it pleased the one who wanted it. Now the Father rests in his will, and is pleased with it.

Nothing happens without him, nor does anything happen without the will of the Father, but his will is incomprehensible. His trace is the will, and no one can know him, nor does he exist for people to scrutinize so that they might grasp him, but when he wills, what he wills is this—even if the sight doesn't please them in any way before God—the will of the Father, because he knows the beginning of all of them, and their end, for in the end he'll greet them directly. Now the end is receiving knowledge of the one who's hidden; this is the Father, **38** from whom the beginning has come, and to whom all who've come out from him will return. They were revealed for the glory and the joy of his name.

CHAP. XIV.

The name of the Father is the Son. Whoever doesn't exist has no name. The Father brought out the Son to disclose his secrets.

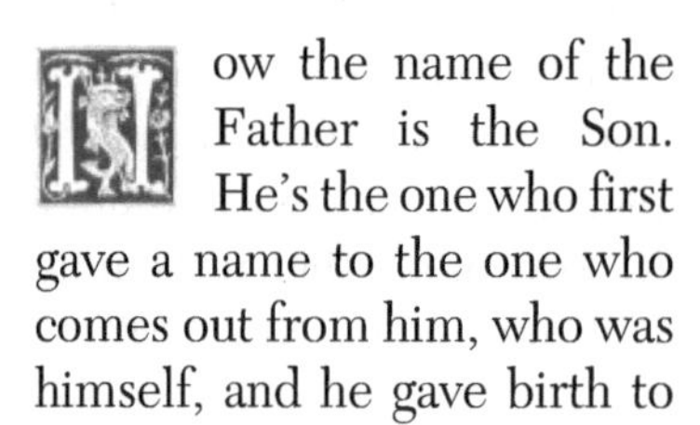

ow the name of the Father is the Son. He's the one who first gave a name to the one who comes out from him, who was himself, and he gave birth to him as a Son. He gave him his name which belonged to him. He's the one to whom everything around the Father belongs. The name and the Son are his. It's possible for him to be seen; the name, however, is invisible, because it alone is the mystery of the invisible which comes to ears that are filled completely with it by him. For indeed, the Father's name isn't spoken, but it's revealed through a Son.

In this way, then, the name is great. Who, then, will be able to utter a name for him, the great name, except him alone to whom the name belongs, and the children of the name, those in whom the Father's name rests, and who themselves, in turn, rest in his name? Since the Father is unbegotten, it's he alone who gave birth to him for himself as a name, before he had made the generations, so that the Father's name might be over their head as Lord, which is the **39** true name, confirmed in his command in complete power. For the name isn't from words and naming; the name, rather, is invisible.

He gave a name to him alone. He alone sees him, he alone having the power to give him a name, because whoever doesn't exist has no name. For what name will they give one who doesn't exist? But the one who exists, exists also with his name, and he alone knows it, and he's given a name to him alone. This is the Father; his name is the Son. He didn't hide it within, then, but it existed. The Son alone gave a name. The name, then, belongs to the Father, as the name of the Father is the beloved Son. Where, indeed, would he find a name, except from the Father?

But doubtless one will ask their neighbor, Who is it who'll give a name to the one who existed before them, as if **40** offspring didn't receive a name from those who gave them birth? First, then, it's right for us to consider what the name is. It's the true name, the name from the Father, because it's the proper name. So he didn't receive the name on loan, the way others do, according to the form in which each one will be produced. This, then, is the proper name. There's no one else who gave it to him. But he's unnameable, indescribable, until the time when he who's complete spoke of him alone. And it's he who has the power to speak his name and to see him.

So when it pleased him that his beloved name should be his Son, and he gave the name to him who came out from the depth, he disclosed his secrets, knowing that the Father is without evil. Because of this, he brought him out so that he might speak about the place, and his resting place from which he had come, **41** and to glorify the fullness, the greatness of his name, and the Father's sweetness.

CHAP. XV.

All have emanated from the Father and will return to their place of rest. The complete one is a Mother for them. They themselves are the Truth, and the Father is in them, and they're in the Father, being complete.

ach one will speak about the place from which they came, and they'll hurry to return again to the place where they received their restoration to receive from the place where they were, receiving a taste from that place and receiving nourishment, receiving growth.

And their place of rest is their fullness. All that have emanated from the Father, then, are fullnesses, and the roots of all that have emanated from him are within the one who caused them all to grow. He gave them their destinies. Then each one was revealed, so that through their own thought [...] for the place to which they send their thought is their root, which takes them up through all the heights, up to the Father. They embrace his head, which is rest for them, and they're grasped, approaching him, as though to say that they receive his expression by means of kisses. But they're not revealed **42** in this way, because they neither exalted themselves, nor wanted the Father's glory, nor did they think of him as trivial or harsh or wrathful; but he's without evil, unperturbed, and sweet. He knows every realm before they've come into existence, and he has no need to be instructed.

This is the way of those who possess something of the immeasurable greatness from above, as they wait for the complete one alone, who's a Mother for them. And they don't go down to Hades, nor do they have envy or groaning, nor death within them, but they rest in the one who rests, not striving nor twisting around in the search for Truth. But they themselves are the Truth, and the Father is within them, and they're in the Father, being complete. They're undivided from the truly good one. They don't need anything, but they rest, refreshed in the Spirit. And they'll listen to their root. They'll devote themselves to those things that they'll find in their root and not suffer loss to their soul. This is the place of the blessed; this is their place.

CHAP. XVII.

Conclusion. The Father is good, and his children are complete.

As for the others, then, may they know, where they're at, that it's not right **43** for me, having come to the place of rest, to say anything else, but I'll come to be in it, and will devote myself continually to the Father of all and the true brothers (and sisters), those upon whom the Father's love is emptied and in whose midst there is no need. They're the ones who are revealed in Truth; they exist in the true eternal life, and they speak of the light that's complete and

that's filled with the Father's seed, and that's in his heart and in the fullness. His Spirit rejoices in it, and glorifies the one in whom it existed, because he's good. And his children are complete, and worthy of his name, because he's the Father. It's children like this that he loves.

THE GOSPEL OF MARY

he Gospel of Mary was originally written in Greek in the second century. It's attested by two third-century Greek fragments discovered in 1938 and 1983, respectively, and one fifth-century Egyptian manuscript first discovered in 1896 but not published until 1955. Unfortunately, over half the Gospel is still missing from the Egyptian manuscript—the first six pages in the beginning, and another four pages in the middle. For more information, see my book, *The Gospel of Mary: A Fresh Translation and Holistic Approach,* published in 2013.

This Gospel is noteworthy as the only Gospel written in the name of a woman, who is portrayed as a leader in the church. Peter's criticism of Mary's authority here is also featured both in the Gospel of Thomas and in the later Pistis Sophia.

The first six pages are missing.

CHAP. I.

Matter is not eternal. Sin doesn't exist in and of itself, but is made by unfaithfulness, which results in sickness and death. Matter gave birth to a passion that has no (heavenly) image. Find contentment in the presence of the various images of nature.

hen will [matter] be [destroyed,] or not?

The Savior said, Every nature, every form, every creature exists in and with each other, but they'll dissolve again into their own roots, because the nature of matter dissolves into its nature alone. Anyone who has ears to hear should hear!

Peter said to him, Since you've explained everything to us, tell us one more thing. What's the sin of the world?

The Savior said, Sin doesn't exist, but you're the ones who make sin when you act in accordance with the nature of unfaithfulness, which is called sin. That's why the Good came among you, up to the things of every nature in order to restore it within its root.

Then he continued and said, That's why you get sick and die, because [you love **8** what tricks you. Anyone who] can understand should understand!

Matter [gave birth to] a passion that has no image because it comes from what's contrary to nature. Then confusion arises in the whole body. That's why I told you to be content at heart. If you're discontented, find contentment in the presence of the various images of nature. Anyone who has ears to hear should hear!

CHAP. II.

The Son of Humanity exists within you. Preach the gospel about the kingdom, but don't lay down extra rules. The disciples grieve and are afraid of the gentiles.

hen the Blessed One said these things, he greeted them all and said, Peace be with you! Acquire my peace. Be careful not to let anyone mislead you by saying, Look over here! or Look over there! Because the Son of Humanity exists within you. Follow him! Those who seek him will find him.

Go then and preach the gospel about the kingdom. Don't **9** lay down any rules beyond what I've given you, nor make a law like the lawgiver, lest you be bound by it. When he said these things, he left.

But they grieved and wept bitterly. They asked, How can we go up to the gentiles to preach the gospel about the kingdom of the Son of Humanity? If they didn't spare him, why would they spare us?

CHAP. III.

Mary comforts the others. Peter asks Mary to share the words of the Savior that they haven't heard. Mary relates a vision she had of the Lord. Mary is blessed because she didn't waver, for where the mind is, there is the treasure.

hen Mary arose and greeted them all. She said to her brothers (and sisters), Don't weep and grieve or let your hearts be divided, because his grace will be with you all and will protect you. Rather we should praise his greatness because

he's prepared us and made us Humans.

When Mary said these things, she turned their hearts [toward] the Good, and they [started] to wrestle over the words of [the Savior.]

10 Peter said to Mary, Sister, we know the Savior loved you more than all other women. Tell us the words of the Savior that you remember —the things which you know that we don't, and which we haven't heard.

In response Mary said, I'll tell you what's hidden from you. So she started to tell them these words: I, she said, I saw the Lord in a vision and said to him, Lord, I saw you in a vision today.

In response he said to me, You're blessed because you didn't waver at the sight of me. For where the mind is, there is the treasure.

I asked him, Lord, now does the one who sees the vision see it <in> the soul <or> in the spirit?

In response the Savior said, They don't see in the soul or in the spirit, but the mind which [exists] between the two is [what] sees the vision [and] it [that …]

Four pages are missing.

CHAP. IV.

The soul ascends past malevolent Powers that seek to bind her.

nd Desire said, I didn't see you going down, but now I see you're going up. So why are you lying, since you belong to me?

In response the soul said, I saw you, but you didn't see me or know me. I was to you just a garment, and you didn't recognize me. When she said these things, she left, rejoicing greatly.

Again, she came to the third power, which is called Ignorance. [It] interrogated the soul and [asked,] Where are you going? In wickedness you're bound. Since you're bound, don't judge!

[And] the soul asked, Why do you judge me, since I haven't judged? I was bound, even though I haven't bound. They didn't recognize me, but I've recognized that everything will dissolve—both the things of the [earth] **16** and the things of [heaven.]

When the soul had overcome the third power, she went up and saw the fourth power, which took seven forms:

Albrecht Altdorfer, The Elevation of Saint Mary Magdalen
Date Unknown
Metropolitan Museum of Art

The first form is Darkness;
The second, Desire;
The third, Ignorance;
The fourth, Zeal for Death;
The fifth, the Kingdom of the Flesh;
The sixth, the Foolish Wisdom of Flesh;
The seventh, the Wisdom of Anger.

These are the seven powers of Wrath.

They ask the soul, Where do you come from, you murderer, and where are you going, conqueror of space?

In response the soul said, What binds me has been killed, what surrounds me has been overcome, my desire is gone, and ignorance has died. In a [world] I was released **17** from a world, [and] in a type from a type which is above, and from the chain of forgetfulness which exists only for a time. From now on I'll receive the rest of the time of the season of the age in silence.

When Mary said these things, she fell silent because the Savior had spoken with her only up to this point.

CHAP. V.

Andrew doubts Mary. Peter wrestles with her like the adversaries (i.e., Powers). Levi rebukes Peter. They start to go out to teach and to preach.

In response Andrew said to the brothers (and sisters), Say what you will about what she's said, I myself don't believe that the Savior said these things, because these teachings seem like different ideas.

In response Peter spoke out with the same concerns. He asked them concerning the Savior: He didn't speak with a woman without our knowledge and not publicly with us, did he? Will we turn around and all listen to her? Did he prefer her to us?

18 Then Mary wept and asked Peter, My brother Peter, what are you thinking? Do you really think that I thought this up by myself in my heart, or that I'm lying about the Savior?

In response Levi said to Peter, Peter, you've always been angry. Now I see you wrestling with this woman like the adversaries. But if the Savior made her worthy, who are you then to reject her? Surely the Savior knows her very well. That's why he loved her more than us.

Rather we should be ashamed, clothe ourselves

with perfect Humanity, acquire it for ourselves as he instructed us, and preach the gospel, not laying down any other rule or other law beyond what the Savior said.

When **19** [Levi said these things,] they started to go out to teach and to preach.

The Gospel According to Mary.

THE BOOK OF THE STRANGER

he Book of the Stranger (or Foreigner) exists only in the fourth-century Egyptian manuscript that also contains the Gospel of Judas. The manuscript was discovered in the 1970s and first published by National Geographic in 2007. Additional fragments published in 2012 have been incorporated into this translation.

This book reflects the temptation and transfiguration narratives of the New Testament Gospels. The most noteworthy feature of this book is its account of Stranger's heavenly ascent past the same malevolent Powers described in the Gospel of Mary.

CHAP. I.

Stranger and his disciple ascend Mount Tabor and pray for God to reveal mysteries.

y [son, let's pray to God ...] to the Father of all the ages, to send us a spirit of knowledge to reveal the mysteries, so that we may know ourselves; specifically, where [we've] come from, where we're going, and what we need to do to live.

And they left and went up on a mountain called Tabor. And they knelt down and prayed, O Lord God, the One above all the great realms, the One who has no beginning and no end, give us a spirit of knowledge to reveal your mysteries, so that we may know ourselves; specifically, where we've come from, where we're going, and what we need to do to live.

CHAP. II.

Satan appears and tempts Stranger, who resists.

fter Stranger had said these words, [Satan] appeared **60** [on] the earth, since he [binds the world.] He said, [...] while you're walking up on this mountain, because although you seek, you won't find anything. But come to me, and [take for] yourself what's in my [world.] Eat my good things. Take for yourself silver, gold, and clothes.

In response Stranger said, Depart from me, Satan, because I don't seek you but my Father, who is above all the great realms; because I've been called Stranger, since I'm from another race. I'm not from your race.

Then the one who binds the [world] told him, We **61** ourselves [...] in my [world.]

[Then] Stranger said to him, Depart from [me,] Satan! Go away, because I don't [belong to] you.

Then Satan [departed] from him, after having angered him many times; and he wasn't able to deceive [him.] And when he had been defeated, he went away to his place in great shame.

CHAP. III.

Stranger is surrounded by a bright cloud and transfigured.

hen Stranger cried out in a loud voice, O God, you who are in the great realms, hear my voice, have mercy on me, and save me from every evil! Look on me and hear me in this deserted place. Now [let your] indescribable [light] shine on me **62** [...] your light. Yes, Lord, help me, because [I] don't know [...] forever and ever.

And while I said these things, look! A bright cloud surrounded me. Because of the way it was shining, I couldn't gaze into the light around it. And I heard something from the cloud and the light. It shone on me and said, O Stranger, the sound of your prayer has been heard, and I've been sent here to tell you the gospel before you leave [this place,] so that **63** you may [know ...] reveal [... body] dissolve [...] the [spirit...]

CHAP. IV.

Instructions on how to ascend past the malevolent Powers.

hen you go, [you'll] come to the first Power, which is the power of Desire. And it will bind you and [ask] you, Where are [you] going, O Stranger? But say, What bound me has been killed, and I've been released. I'll go

Albrecht Altdorfer, The Transfiguration of Christ, ca. 1513
Metropolitan Museum of Art

up to my Father, the One above all the great realms. And it will release you.

Then you'll come to the second Power, which is the power of Darkness. [And it] will bind [you and] **64** [ask you,] Where [are you going, O Stranger? But say, What bound me has been killed, and I've been released. I'll go up to my Father, the One above all the great realms. Then it will release you.]

[And you'll] come to the [third] Power, which is called Ignorance. It will bind you and say to you, Where [are you going, O] Stranger? But say to it, What bound me has been killed, and I've been released. I'll go up to my Father, the One above all the great realms. Then it will release you.

And you'll come to the fourth Power, which [... Death. It will say to you, Where are you going, O Stranger?] **65** [But say, What bound me has been killed, and I've been released. I'll go up to my Father, the One above all the great realms. And it will release you.]

[And you'll come to the fifth] Power, [which is the] Kingdom [of the] Flesh. [And it will] say to you, [Where are] you [going, O Stranger? But say, What bound] me has been [killed,] and I've [been] released. [Now] then, I'll go up to my Father, [the One] above [all the great realms. And it will] release you.

[And you'll come to the sixth Power, which is the Foolish] Wisdom [of Flesh. And] it will say to you, Where [are you going,] O [Stranger]? But say to [it, What] bound me [has been killed, and I've been released. I'll go up to my Father,] **66** [the One above all the great realms. And it will release you.]

[…] in […] and you'll [go up] over [these] angels […] myriads of [holy] angels [… myriads of] angels […] Don't be faint of heart […] Be strong [... O Stranger,] because you […] Don't be afraid […] which was said […]

An unknown number of pages is missing.

CHAP. V.

Conclusion.

tranger […] he sent […] so that they might [… the] judgment. [Peace to the one] who wrote them down [and to those who will] preserve them.

THE GOSPEL OF JUDAS

The Gospel of Judas was originally written in Greek in the second century, but currently exists only in a fourth-century Egyptian translation that was discovered in the 1970s and first published by National Geographic in 2007. Additional fragments published in 2010 have been incorporated into this translation. For more information, see my book, *The Gospel of Judas: The Sarcastic Gospel,* published in 2014.

Scholars agree that this Gospel's caustic portrayal of Jesus' twelve disciples (who are portrayed as worse off than Judas Iscariot) functions as a thinly-veiled criticism of second-century Church leaders.

CHAP. I.

Jesus spoke a secret message of judgment with Judas Iscariot.

This is the secret message of judgment Jesus spoke with Judas Iscariot over a period of eight days, three days before he celebrated Passover.

When he appeared on earth, he did signs and great wonders for the salvation of humanity. Some [walked] in the way of righteousness, but others walked in their transgression, so the twelve disciples were called. He started to tell them about the mysteries beyond the world and what would happen at the end. Often he didn't reveal himself to his disciples, but you'd find him in their midst as a child.

CHAP. II.

Jesus laughs at the disciples' practice of prayer. His disciples become furious. Only Judas is strong enough to stand before Jesus, who will tell him the mysteries of the kingdom.

One day he was with his disciples in Judea. He found them sitting together practicing their piety.

When he [came up to] his disciples **34** sitting together praying over the bread, [he] laughed.

The disciples asked him, Master, why are you laughing at [our] prayer? What have we done? [This] is what's right.

In response he said to them, I'm not laughing at you. You're not doing this because you want to, but because through this your God [will be] praised.

They said, Master, you [...] are the Son of our God!

Jesus asked them, How do [you] know me? Truly [I] say to you, no generation of the people among you will know me.

When his disciples heard this, [they] started to get angry and furious and started to curse him in their hearts.

But when Jesus noticed their ignorance, [he asked] them, Why are you letting your anger trouble you? Has your God within you and [his stars] **35** become angry with your souls? If any of you is [strong enough] among humans to bring out the perfect Humanity, stand up and face me.

All of them said, We're strong enough. But their spirits weren't brave enough to stand before [him]—except Judas Iscariot. He was able to stand before him, but he couldn't look him in the eye, so he looked away.

Judas [said] to him, I know who you are and where you've come from. You've come from the immortal realm of Barbelo, and I'm not worthy to utter the name of the one who's sent you.

Then Jesus, knowing that he was thinking about what's exalted, said to him, Come away from the others and I'll tell you the mysteries of the kingdom. Not so that you'll go there, but you'll grieve much **36** because someone else will replace you to complete the twelve [elements] before their God.

Judas asked him, When will you tell me these things, and when will the great day of light dawn for the generation [...]?

But when he said these things, Jesus left him.

CHAP. III.

Jesus tells his disciples about another great and holy generation. His disciples are troubled.

The next morning, he appeared to his disciples. [And] they

asked him, Master, where did [you] go, and what did you do when you left us?

Jesus said to them, I went to another great and holy generation.

His disciples asked him, Lord, what great generation is better and holier than us, that's not in these realms?

Now when Jesus heard this, he laughed. He asked them, Why are you wondering in your hearts about the strong and holy generation? **37** Truly I say to you, no one born [of] this realm will see that [generation,] no army of angels from the stars will rule over it, and no person of mortal birth will be able to join it, because that generation doesn't come from [...] that has become [...] the generation of the people among [them] is from the generation of the great people [...] the powerful authorities who [...] nor the powers [...] those by which you rule.

When his disciples heard these things, they were each troubled in their spirit. They couldn't say a thing.

CHAP. IV.

Jesus' disciples narrate a troubling dream about a Temple with twelve corrupt priests. Jesus explains that they are the priests they have dreamed about. Jesus tells them to stop sacrificing animals.

Another day Jesus came up to them. They said to him, Master, we've seen you in a dream, because we had great [dreams last] night.

But Jesus asked, Why [...] hidden yourselves?

38 And they [said, We saw] a great [house, with a great] altar [in it, and] twelve people—we'd say they were priests—and a name. And a crowd of people was waiting at the altar [until] the priests [finished receiving] the offerings. We kept waiting too.

[Jesus asked,] What were they like?

And they said, [Some] fast [for] two weeks. Others sacrifice their own children; others their wives, praising and humbling themselves among each other. Others sleep around with men; others murder; yet others commit many sins and do criminal things. [And] the people standing [before] the altar invoke your [name!] **39** And in all their sacrificing, they fill the [altar] with their offerings. When they said this, [they] fell silent, because they were troubled.

Jesus asked them, Why are you troubled? Truly I say to you, all the priests standing before that altar invoke my name. And [again,] I say to you, my name has been written on this [house] of the generations of the stars by the human generations. [And they] have shamefully planted fruitless trees in my name.

Jesus (further) said to them, You're the ones receiving the offerings on the altar you've seen. That's the God you serve, and you're the twelve people you've seen. And the animals you saw brought in to be sacrificed are the crowd you lead astray **40** before that altar. [Your minister] will stand up and use my name like that, and [the] generations of the pious will be loyal to him. After him, another person will present [those who sleep around,] and another those who murder children, and another those who sleep around with men, and those who fast, and the rest of impurity, crime, and error. And those who say, We're equal to the angels—they're the stars that finish everything. It's been said to the human generations, Look, God has accepted your sacrifice from the hands of priests, that is, the minister of error. But the Lord who commands is the Lord over everything. On the last day, they'll be found guilty.

41 Jesus said [to them,] Stop [sacrificing animals.] You've [offered them] over the altar, over your stars with your angels where they've already been completed. So let them become [...] with you and let them [become] clear.

His disciples [said to him,] Cleanse us from our [sins] that we've committed through the deceit of the angels.

Jesus said to them, It's not possible [...] nor [can] a fountain quench the fire of the entire inhabited world. Nor can a [city's] well satisfy all the generations, except the great, stable one. A single lamp won't illuminate all the realms, except the second generation, nor can a baker feed all creation **42** under [heaven.]

And [when the disciples heard] these [things,] they said to [him,] Master, help us and save us!

Jesus said to them, Stop struggling against me. Each one of you has (your) own star, [and ...] of the stars will [...] what belongs to it [...] I wasn't sent to the corruptible generation, but to the strong and incorruptible generation, because no enemy has ruled [over] that generation, nor any of the stars. Truly I say to you, the pillar of fire will fall quickly and that generation won't be moved by the stars.

CHAP. V.

Jesus takes Judas aside and explains the human generations.

nd when Jesus [said] these things, he left, [taking] Judas Iscariot with him. He said to him, The water on the exalted mountain is [from] **43** [...] it didn't come to [water ... the well] of the tree of [the fruit ...] of this realm [...] after a time [...] but came to water God's paradise and the enduring [fruit,] because [it] won't corrupt that generation's [walk of life,] but [it will exist] for all eternity.

Judas said to [him, Tell] me what kind of fruit this generation has.

Jesus said, The souls of every human generation will die; however, when these people have completed the time in the kingdom and the spirit leaves them, their bodies will die but their souls will live, and they'll be taken up.

Judas asked, What will the rest of the human generations do?

Jesus said, It's not possible **44** to sow on [rock] and harvest its fruit. In the same way, it's [not possible to sow on] the [defiled] race along with the perishable wisdom [and] the hand which created mortal humans so that their souls may go up to the realms above. [Truly] I say to you, [no ruler,] angel, [or] power will be able to see the [places] that [this great,] holy generation [will see.] When Jesus said this, he left.

CHAP. VI.

Judas narrates his dream about a Temple. Jesus explains that holy place so that Judas can grieve when he sees the holy generation enter it without him.

udas said, Master, just as you've listened to all of them, now listen to me too, because I've seen a great vision.

But Jesus laughed when he heard this. He asked him, Why are you all worked up, you thirteenth demon? But speak up, and I'll bear with you.

Judas said to him, In the vision, I saw myself. The twelve disciples are stoning me and **45** chasing [me rapidly]. And I also came to the place where [I had followed] you. I saw [a house in this place,] and my eyes couldn't [measure] its size. Great people surrounded it, and that house had a roof of greenery. In the middle of the house was [a crowd …] Master, take me in with these people!

In response [Jesus] said, Your star has led you astray, Judas, and no person of mortal birth is worthy to enter the house you've seen, because that place is reserved for those who are holy. Neither the sun nor the moon will rule there, nor the day, but those who are holy will always stand in the realm with the holy angels. Look, I've told you the mysteries of the kingdom **46** and I've taught you about the error of the stars and […] sent [on high] over the twelve realms.

Judas asked, Master, surely my offspring don't dominate the rulers, do they?

In response Jesus said to him, Come, let me [tell] you [about the holy generation. Not so that you'll go there,] but you'll grieve much when you see the kingdom and all its generation.

When Judas heard this, he asked him, What good has it done me that you've separated me from that generation?

In response Jesus said, You'll become the thirteenth, and will be cursed by the other generations and will rule over them. In the last days they'll […] to you and you won't go up **47** to the holy generation.

CHAP. VII.

Jesus reveals mysteries to Judas, narrating the process of creation. Saklas and his angels created human beings. God commanded Michael to loan spirits to people to serve, and commanded Gabriel to give spirits to the great generation with no king. God caused knowledge to be brought to Adam. The rulers and their creations will be destroyed.

esus said, [Come] and I'll teach you about the [mysteries that no] human [will] see, because there exists a great and boundless realm whose horizons no angelic generation has seen, [in] which is a [great] invisible Spirit, which no [angelic] eye has ever seen, no heart has ever comprehended, and it's never been called by any name.

And a luminous cloud appeared there. And (the Spirit) said, Let an angel come into being to attend me. And a great angel, the Self-Begotten, the God of the Light, emerged from the cloud. And because of him, another four angels came into being from another cloud, and they attended the angelic Self-Begotten. And said **48** the [Self-Begotten,] Let [a realm] come into being, and it came into being [just as he said.] And he [created] the first luminary to rule over it. And he said, Let angels come into being to serve [it, and] countless [myriads] came into being. And he said, [Let a] luminous realm come into being, and it came into being. He created the second luminary to rule over it, along with countless myriads of angels to offer service. And that's how he created the rest of the realms of light. And he made them to be ruled, and created for them countless myriads of angels to assist them.

And Adamas was in the first cloud of light that no angel could ever see among all those called God. **49** And [Adamas begat Seth in] that [place after the] image [of ...] and after the likeness of [this] angel. He made the incorruptible [generation] of Seth appear to the twelve androgynous [luminaries. And then] he made seventy-two luminaries appear in the incorruptible generation according to the Spirit's will. Then the seventy-two luminaries themselves made three hundred sixty luminaries appear in the incorruptible generation according to the Spirit's will so that there'd be five for each. And the twelve realms of the twelve luminaries make up their father, with six heavens for each realm so there are seventy-two heavens for the seventy-two luminaries, and for each one **50** [of them five] firmaments [for a total of] three hundred sixty [firmaments. They] were given authority and a [great] army of countless angels for honor and service, along with virgin spirits [too] for the honor and [service] of all the realms and the heavens with their firmaments.

Now the crowd of those immortals is called cosmos—that is, perishable—by the father and the seventy-two luminaries with the Self-Begotten and his seventy-two realms. That's where the first human appeared with his incorruptible powers. In the realm that appeared with his generation is the cloud of knowledge and the angel who's called **51** [Eleleth …] After these things [Eleleth] said, Let twelve angels come into being [to] rule over Chaos and [Hades.] And look, from the cloud there appeared an [angel] whose face flashed with [fire] and whose likeness was [defiled] by blood. His name was Nebro, which means Rebel. Others call him Yaldabaoth. And another angel, Saklas, came from the cloud too. So Nebro created six angels—and Saklas (did too)—to be assistants. They brought out twelve angels in the heavens, with each of them receiving a portion in the heavens.

And the twelve rulers spoke with the twelve angels: Let each of you **52** […] and let them […] generation [… five] angels:

The first [is Yaoth], who's called the Good One. The second is Harmathoth, [the eye of fire.] The [third] is Galila. The fourth [is] Yobel. The fifth is Adonaios. These are the five who ruled over Hades and are the first over Chaos.

Then Saklas said to his angels, Let's create a human being after the likeness and the image. And they fashioned Adam and his wife Eve, who in the cloud is called Life, because by this name all the generations seek him, and each of them calls her by their names. Now Saklas didn't **53** [command …] give birth, except […] among the generations […] which this […] and the [angel] said to him, Your life will last for a limited time, with your children.

Then Judas asked Jesus, [How] long can a person live?

Jesus asked, Why are you amazed that the lifespans of Adam and his generation are limited in the place he's received his kingdom with his ruler?

Judas asked Jesus, Does the human spirit die?

Jesus said, This is how it is. God commanded Michael to loan spirits to people so that they might serve. Then the Great One commanded Gabriel to give spirits to the great generation with no king—the spirit along with the soul. So the [rest] of the souls **54** […] light [… the] Chaos […] seek [the] spirit within you which you've made to live in this flesh from the angelic generations. Then God caused knowledge to be brought to Adam and those with him, so that the kings of Chaos and Hades might not rule over them.

[Then] Judas asked Jesus, So what will those generations do?

Jesus said, Truly I say to you, the stars complete all these things. When Saklas completes the time span that's been determined for him, their first star will appear with the generations, and they'll finish what's been said. Then they'll sleep around in my name, murder their children, **55** and [they'll …] evil and […] the realms, bringing the generations and presenting them to Saklas. [And] after that […] will bring the twelve tribes of [Israel] from […] and the [generations] will all serve Saklas, sinning in my name. And your star will [rule] over the thirteenth realm. Then Jesus [laughed.]

[Judas] asked, Master, why [are you laughing at me?]

In response [Jesus said], I'm not laughing [at you but] at the error of the stars, because these six stars go astray with these five warriors, and they'll all be destroyed along with their creations.

CHAP. VIII.

Judas' heart strays, and he sacrifices the humanity that bears Jesus.

Then Judas asked Jesus, What will those do who've been baptized in your name?

Jesus said, Truly I say [to you,] this baptism **56** [which they've received in] my name […] will destroy the whole generation of the earthly Adam. Tomorrow they'll torture the one who bears me. Truly I [say] to you, no hand of a mortal human [will fall] upon me. Truly [I say] to you, Judas, those who offer sacrifices to Saklas […] everything that's evil. But you'll do more than all of them, because you'll sacrifice the human who bears me. Your horn has already been raised, your anger has been kindled, your star has ascended, and your heart has [strayed.] **57** Truly [I say to you,] your last [… and] the [… the thrones] of the realm have [been defeated,] the kings have grown weak, the angelic generations have grieved, and the evil [they sowed …] is destroyed, [and] the [ruler] is wiped out. [And] then the [fruit] of the great generation of Adam will

Albrecht Altdorfer, The Betrayal of Christ, 1508
Museum of Fine Arts, Houston

be exalted, because before heaven, earth, and the angels, that generation from the realms exists. Look, you've been told everything. Lift up your eyes and see the cloud with the light in it and the stars around it. And the star that leads the way is your star.

Then Judas looked up and saw the luminous cloud, and he entered it. Those standing on the ground heard a voice from the cloud. It said, **58** [… the] great [generation …] and […] and Judas didn't see Jesus anymore.

Immediately there was a disturbance among [the] Jews, more than […] Their high priests grumbled because he'd gone into the guest room to pray. But some scribes were there watching closely so they could arrest him during his prayer, because they were afraid of the people, since they all regarded him as a prophet.

And they approached Judas and asked him, What are you doing here? Aren't you Jesus' disciple?

Then he answered them as they wished. Then Judas received some money and handed him over to them.

The Gospel of Judas.

Infancy Gospels

THE INFANCY GOSPEL OF JAMES

he Infancy Gospel of James was originally written in the second century. Manuscripts have survived in many languages, but most—around 140 manuscripts—are written in Greek (with varying titles).

Scholars have divided the manuscripts into five families. The most important manuscript is the Papyrus Bodmer V, which has been dated to the late third or early fourth century. It was unknown at the time of Tischendorf's nineteenth-century transcript, which was the basis for many earlier translations. This translation is principally based on the critical text of Émile de Strycker. For more information, see my book, *The Infancy Gospels: Exploring Jesus' Family,* published in 2019.

Despite its popularity and far-reaching impact in Christian history, this Gospel fell out of favor because it portrays Jesus' siblings as children of Joseph from a prior marriage instead of as first cousins.

CHAP. I.

1 *Joachim, a rich man, offers to the Lord,* 2 *is opposed by Reubel because he has not had a child in Israel,* 4 *retires into the wilderness, and fasts forty days and forty nights.*

n the histories of the twelve tribes of Israel, Joachim was a very rich man. And he doubled the gifts he offered to the Lord. He said to himself, One is from my surplus for all the people, and the other is to the Lord God for forgiveness, to atone for me.

2 Now the great day of the Lord was approaching, and the people of Israel were offering their gifts. But Reubel stood before him and said, It's not right for you to offer your gifts first, since you haven't had a child in Israel.

3 And Joachim was very grieved and went to the (history) of the twelve tribes of the people, saying to himself, I'll look in the (history) of the twelve tribes of Israel to see

whether I'm the only one who hasn't had a child in Israel. And he searched, and found that all the just people in Israel had raised children. And he remembered that in the last days of the patriarch Abraham, the Lord God gave him a son, Isaac.

4 And Joachim was very grieved, and didn't go to his wife, but gave himself to the wilderness and pitched his tent there. And Joachim fasted forty days and forty nights. He said to himself, I won't go down for food or drink until the Lord my God considers me. Prayer will be my food and drink.

CHAP. II.

1 *Anna, the wife of Joachim, mourns her infertility,* 2 *is blamed for it by Juthine her servant,* 4 *sits under a laurel tree, and prays to the Lord.*

ow his wife, Anna, mourned and lamented for two reasons. She said, I lament that I'm (virtually) a widow and that I don't have a child.

2 Now the great day of the Lord was approaching, and her servant Juthine asked her, How long are you going to humiliate your soul? Look, the great day of the Lord has approached, and it's not right for you to grieve. But take this headband which the leader of the workplace gave me. It's not right for me to wear it, since I'm your servant, and it has a royal mark.

3 And Anna said, Get away from me! I won't do this. The Lord God has greatly humiliated me. Maybe a trickster gave this to you, and you've come to get me to share in your sin.

And Juthine the servant asked, Why should I curse you, since you haven't heard my voice? The Lord God has made your womb infertile, to give you no fruit in Israel.

4 And Anna was very grieved, and removed her garment of mourning, washed her head, and put on her wedding garment. And at about the ninth hour she went down into her garden to walk around. She saw a laurel tree and sat down under it. And after resting, she petitioned the Lord. She said, God of my ancestors, bless me and hear my prayer, as you blessed our mother Sarah and gave her a son, Isaac.

CHAP. III.

1 *Seeing a sparrow's nest in the laurel tree, Anna laments her infertility.*

nna looked intently to heaven and saw a nest of sparrows in the laurel tree. And Anna lamented. She said to herself:

Woe is me! Who gave birth to me? What womb bore me? I was born as a curse before the people of Israel and have been despised; they've mocked me and banished me from the Temple of the Lord my God.

2 Woe is me! What am I like? I'm not like the birds of heaven, because even the birds of heaven are fruitful before you, Lord.

Woe is me! What am I like? I'm not like the animals, because even the animals are fruitful before you, Lord.

Woe is me! What am I like? I'm not like the wild beasts of the earth, because even the wild beasts of the earth are fruitful before you, Lord.

3 Woe is me! What am I like? I'm not like these waters, because even these waters are serene yet churn, and their fish bless you, Lord.

Woe is me! What am I like? I'm not like this earth, because the earth produces her fruits when it's time and blesses you, Lord.

CHAP. IV.

1 *An angel appears to Anna and tells her she'll conceive.* 2 *An angel appears to Joachim.* 3 *Joachim sacrifices.* 4 *Anna goes to meet him, rejoicing that she will conceive. Joachim rests for the first day in his house.*

nd look! An angel of the Lord stood nearby. It said to her, Anna, Anna, the Lord has heard your prayer. You'll conceive and give birth, and your offspring will be spoken of through the whole world.

And Anna said, As the Lord God lives, whether I give birth to a boy or a girl, I'll bring it as a gift to the Lord my God, and it'll minister to him all the days of its life.

2 And look! Two angels came and said to her, Look, Joachim, your husband, is coming with his flocks. For an angel of the Lord had gone down to Joachim and said, Joachim, Joachim, the Lord God has heard your prayer. Go down from here. Look, your

Albrecht Altdorfer, Meeting of Joachim
and Anna at the Golden Gate, ca. 1513
Metropolitan Museum of Art

wife, Anna, has conceived in her womb.

3 And immediately Joachim went down and called the shepherds. He said to them, Bring here to me ten lambs without spot or blemish, and the ten lambs will be for the Lord God. And bring me twelve tender calves for the priests and the elders. And a hundred male goats for all the people.

4 And look! Joachim came with his flocks, and Anna stood at the gate. And she saw Joachim coming with his flocks, and immediately ran and flung herself around his neck and said, Now I know that the Lord God has greatly blessed me. For look! The widow is no longer a widow, and look! The one without a child in her womb has conceived.

And Joachim rested for the first day in his house.

CHAP. V.

1 *Joachim sacrifices, consults the plate worn by the priest, and is without sin.* 2 *Anna gives birth to a daughter, whom she names Mary.*

nd the next day, he was offering his gifts. He said to himself, If the Lord God is reconciled to me, the plate worn by the priest will make it clear to me. And Joachim offered his gifts and paid attention to the priest's plate as he went up to the altar of the Lord. And he didn't see sin in it. And Joachim said, Now I know that the Lord God has been reconciled to me and has sent all my sins away from me. And he went down from the Temple of the Lord justified and went into his house.

2 And about six months were completed, and in the seventh month she gave birth. And Anna asked her midwife, What is it?

And the midwife said, It's a girl!

And Anna said, My soul is magnified this day! And she laid down her child.

And when her days were completed, Anna cleansed her flow of blood. And she gave her breast to the child, and gave her the name Mary.

CHAP. VI.

1 *At six months old, Mary walks seven steps. Anna keeps her holy.* 2 *When she is a year old, Joachim makes a great feast.* 3 *Anna breastfeeds her and sings a song to the Lord God.*

nd day by day, the child grew stronger. When she was six months old, her mother stood her on the ground to test whether she could stand. And walking seven steps, she came to her mother's breast, and her mother caught her up and said, As the Lord my God lives, you won't walk on this ground again until I bring you into the Temple of the Lord.

And she made a sanctuary in her bedroom and didn't allow anything sacrilegious or impure to pass through it. And she called the pure daughters of the Hebrews, and they played with her.

2 And when the child grew to be a year old, Joachim made a great feast, and called the chief priests, and the priests, and the scribes, and the elders, and all the people of Israel. And Joachim brought the child to the priests, and they blessed her. They said, God of our ancestors, bless this child and give her a name that'll be spoken forever among all generations.

And all the people said, So be it. Amen!

And they brought her to the chief priests, and they blessed her. They said, Most High God, look upon this child, and bless her with a final blessing which can't be surpassed.

3 And her mother took her up to the sanctuary of her bedroom and gave her breast to the child. And Anna made a song to the Lord God. She sang:

I'll sing a holy song to the Lord my God, because God has visited me, and has removed the criticism of my enemies.

And the Lord God has given me the fruit of his justice, singular yet manifold before him.

Who will report to Reubel's people that Anna nurses a child? Listen, listen, twelve tribes of Israel: Anna nurses a child!

And Anna rested in the sanctuary of her bedroom. And she went and ministered to them. When dinner was finished, they went down rejoicing and glorifying the God of Israel.

CHAP. VII.

2 *When Mary is three years old, Joachim calls the pure daughters of the Hebrews to light their lamps and go with her to the temple.* 3 *The priest places her on the third step of the altar and she dances on her feet.*

Albrecht Altdorfer, The Virgin Entering the Temple, ca. 1513
Metropolitan Museum of Art

nd she cared for her child through the months. When she was two years old, Joachim said, Let's take her to the Temple of the Lord, so that we may keep the promise we made, so that the Lord won't be angry with us and find our gift unacceptable.

But Anna said, Let's wait until her third year, so that she won't seek her father or mother.

And Joachim said, Let's wait.

2 And the child turned three years old, and Joachim said, Let's call the pure daughters of the Hebrews. And let them take their lamps, and let them be lit, so that the child won't turn back, and her heart won't be drawn away from the Temple of the Lord. And they did so until they went up to the Temple of the Lord.

And the priest welcomed her, kissed her, and said, The Lord God has magnified your name among all the generations. Through you, the Lord will reveal his redemption of the people of Israel in the last days.

3 And he sat her down on the third step of the altar, and the Lord God poured grace upon her. And she danced on her feet, and all the house of Israel loved her.

CHAP. VIII.

1 *Mary fed in the temple by an angel.* 2 *When she is twelve years old, the priests discuss what to do.* 3 *An angel of the Lord instructs Zechariah to assemble the widowers, each bearing a staff. The men rush in at the sound of the trumpet.*

nd her parents went down, marveling and praising and glorifying the Lord God that the child hadn't turned back. And Mary was in the Temple of the Lord. She was nurtured like a dove, and received food from the hand of an angel.

2 And when she turned twelve years old, there was a council of the priests. They said, Look, Mary has been in the Temple of the Lord twelve years. What should we do about her so that she won't (ritually) pollute the sanctuary of the Lord our God? And they said to the chief priest, Stand at the altar of the Lord. Go in and pray about her, and if the Lord God reveals anything to you, we'll do it.

3 And the chief priest went in, taking the robe with twelve

bells into the Holy of Holies, and prayed about her. And look! An angel of the Lord stood nearby and said, Zechariah, Zechariah, go out and assemble the widowers of the people, and let them each bear a staff. And whomever the Lord God points out with a sign, she'll be his wife.

And the heralds went down through the whole surrounding area of Judea, and sounded the trumpet of the Lord. And look! All the men rushed in.

CHAP. IX.

1 *Joseph throws down his axe and goes to the meeting. A dove goes out from his staff and flies upon his head. He is chosen to marry the virgin.* 2 *He refuses because he is an old man, but is compelled.* 3 *He takes her home and goes to build houses.*

nd Joseph threw down his axe, and went to their meeting. And when they had all gathered, they went to the priest with their staffs. And having taken all their staffs, he went into the Temple and prayed. And when he had finished the prayer, he took the staffs, went out, and gave them back. But there wasn't a sign among them. And Joseph took his staff last, and look! A dove went out from the staff, and flew upon Joseph's head. And the priest said to Joseph, You've been chosen to welcome the virgin of the Lord into your own care.

2 But Joseph refused. He said, I have sons and am an old man, but she's young. I won't be a laughingstock among the people of Israel.

And the priest said, Joseph, fear the Lord your God, and remember what God did to Dathan, Abiron, and Kore; how the earth opened and swallowed them all because of their rebellion. And now be afraid, Joseph, so that these things won't happen in your house.

3 And being afraid, Joseph welcomed her into his care, and said to her, Mary, I've taken you from the Temple of the Lord, and now I bring you to my house. I'm going away to build houses, but I'll come back to you. The Lord will protect you.

CHAP. X.

1 *The priests desire a new veil for the temple,* 2 *seven virgins cast lots for making different parts of it, and the lot*

to spin the true purple falls to Mary. Zechariah the chief priest falls silent.

nd there was a council of the priests. They said, Let's make a veil for the Temple of the Lord.

And the priest said, Call the pure virgins from the tribe of David to me. And the officers went out and searched and found seven. And the priest remembered that the child Mary was from the tribe of David and pure before God. And the officers went out and brought her.

2 And they brought them into the Temple of the Lord, and the priest said, Cast lots for me to see who will spin the gold and the white and the linen and the silk and the violet and the scarlet and the true purple. And the lot for the true purple and scarlet fell to Mary. And she took them into her house. This was the time that Zechariah fell silent, and Samuel took his place until Zechariah could speak. And Mary took the scarlet and was spinning it.

CHAP. XI.

1 *Mary takes a pitcher to draw water, hears a voice, trembles, and begins to work.* 2 *An angel appears, salutes her,* 3 *and tells her she will conceive by the power of God. She consents.*

nd she took the pitcher and went to fill it with water, and look! A voice said to her, Rejoice, blessed one! The Lord is with you. Blessed are you among women.

And Mary looked around to the right and the left, to see where the voice might be coming from. And she became terrified and went into her house. And setting down the pitcher, she took up the purple and sat upon her throne and spun the purple.

2 And look! An angel of the Lord stood before her and said, Don't be afraid, Mary, because you've found grace before the Lord of All. You'll conceive from God's word.

And hearing this, Mary questioned herself. She said, Will I conceive from the Lord, the living God, and give birth like all women give birth?

3 And the angel of the Lord said to her, Not like that, Mary, because the power of God will overshadow you, so the holy one who will be born from you will be called the

Son of the Most High. And you'll call his name Jesus, because he'll save his people from their sins.

And Mary said, Look, I'm the servant of the Lord. May it be to me according to your word.

CHAP. XII.

1 *Mary takes the purple and the scarlet to the priest.* 2 *Mary visits her cousin Elizabeth, whose child leaps in her womb.*

nd she made the purple and the scarlet, and she took it to the priest. And taking it, the priest blessed her and said, Mary, the Lord God has magnified your name, and you'll be blessed among all the generations of the earth.

2 And Mary rejoiced and went to her cousin Elizabeth. And she knocked at the door. And Elizabeth heard, flung down the scarlet, and rushed to the door. And she opened it and blessed her and asked, How is it that the mother of my Lord should come to me? Because look, the one in me leaped and blessed you!

But Mary forgot the mysteries which Gabriel the angel had told her. And she looked intently into heaven and asked, Lord, who am I, that all the women of the earth will bless me?

3 And she spent three months with Elizabeth. And day by day, her womb grew larger, and Mary was afraid. She went to her house and hid herself from the people of Israel. She was sixteen years old when these mysteries happened to her.

CHAP. XIII.

1 *Joseph returns from building, finds Mary six months pregnant, is jealous and troubled,* 2 *and reproaches her.* 3 *She affirms her innocence.*

nd she was in her sixth month. And look! Joseph came from his building, and came into the house, and found her pregnant. And he struck his face and flung himself on the ground in sackcloth, wept bitterly, and said, How can I look to the Lord God? What prayer can I say about this young girl, since I took her as a virgin from the Temple of the Lord God and didn't protect her? Who has set this trap for me? Who has done this evil thing in my house? Who has defiled the virgin? Aren't I reliving the story of Adam? For as Adam was glorifying in the hour of prayer, the serpent came, found Eve alone, and deceived her, and now it's happened to me!

2 And Joseph stood from the sackcloth and called her and said to her, God cared for you. Why have you done this? You've forgotten the Lord your God. Why have you humiliated your soul? You were nourished in the Holy of Holies and received food from the hand of an angel!

3 And she wept bitterly. She said, I'm pure, and I haven't known a man!

And Joseph asked her, Where then did this thing in your womb come from?

And she said, As the Lord my God lives, I don't know where it came from!

CHAP. XIV.

1 *Joseph determines to dismiss her privately,* 2 *is warned in a dream that Mary is pregnant by the Holy Spirit, and glorifies God who has shown such grace.*

nd Joseph was very afraid and kept quiet about her, considering what to do about her. And Joseph said, If I hide her sin, I'll be found resisting the Law of the Lord, but if I reveal her to the people of Israel, I'm afraid that what's inside her might be angelic, and I'll be found handing over innocent blood to the judgment of death. So what will I do about her? I'll secretly set her free from me. And night overtook him.

2 And look! An angel of the Lord appeared to him in a dream. It said, Don't fear this child, for the one in her is from the Holy Spirit. And she'll give birth to a son, and you'll call his name Jesus, because he'll save his people from their sins.

And Joseph arose from his sleep and glorified the God of Israel, who had given grace to him. And he protected her.

CHAP. XV.

1 *Annas visits Joseph, sees Mary pregnant,* 2 *and tells the priest that Joseph has acted lawlessly. Joseph and Mary are brought to trial on the charge.*

nd Annas the scribe came to him and asked him, Joseph,

why haven't you appeared among our traveling group?

And he said to him, Because I was weary from the trip and rested the first day back.

And Annas turned and saw Mary pregnant.

2 And he quickly went to the priest and said to him, Joseph, about whom you bore witness, has acted very lawlessly.

And the priest asked, What's this?

And he said, The virgin that Joseph took from the Temple of the Lord, he's defiled her and has stolen her wedding and hasn't revealed it to the people of Israel.

And in response the priest asked, Has Joseph done this?

And Annas the scribe said to him, Send officers, and you'll find the virgin pregnant.

And the officers went and found her just as he said. And they led her together with Joseph to the court.

3 And the chief priest asked her, Mary, why have you done this? Why have you humiliated your soul and forgotten the Lord your God? You were raised in the Holy of Holies, and received food from the hand of an angel, and you heard its hymns and danced before it. What is this that you've done?

And she wept bitterly. She said, As the Lord God lives, I'm pure before God, and I haven't known a man!

4 And the priest asked, Joseph, what is this that you've done?

And Joseph said, As the Lord my God lives, and the witness of God's truth, I'm pure toward her.

And the priest said, Don't bear false witness, but tell the truth. You stole her wedding and didn't reveal it to the people of Israel, and you haven't bowed your head under the mighty hand that should bless your offspring.

And Joseph fell silent.

CHAP. XVI.

1 *The chief priest orders trial by the water of the Lord's rebuke.* 2 *Joseph and Mary drink the water, and receiving no harm,* 3 *return home.*

nd the priest said, Return the virgin you took from the Temple of the Lord.

And Joseph was tearful.

And the chief priest said, I'll give you the water of the Lord's rebuke to drink, and it'll reveal your sin in your eyes.

2 And taking (the water), the priest gave it to Joseph and sent him into the wilderness. And Joseph returned unharmed.

And he gave it to Mary and sent her into the wilderness. And she returned unharmed.

And all the people were amazed that their sin wasn't revealed.

3 And the priest said, If the Lord God hasn't revealed your sin to you, neither do I judge you. And he set them free.

And Joseph took Mary and went to his house, rejoicing and glorifying the God of Israel.

CHAP. XVII.

1 *An order goes out from Augustus to register the people of Bethlehem.* 2 *Joseph puts Mary on a donkey to return to Bethlehem. She looks sad, then laughs. Joseph asks why. She tells him she sees two people, one crying and the other rejoicing.* 3 *The delivery being near, he takes her from the donkey.*

ow an order went out from Augustus the king to register how many people were in Bethlehem of Judea.

And Joseph said, I'll register my sons. But what should I do about this child? How will I register her? As my wife? I'm ashamed. As my daughter? But the people of Israel know she's not my daughter. This is the day of the Lord; I'll do whatever the Lord wants.

2 And he saddled the donkey, and sat her on it, and his son led it, and Samuel followed.

And as they neared the third mile, Joseph turned and saw that she was sad. And he was saying, Likely the one inside her is troubling her.

And again Joseph turned and saw her laughing, and he asked her, Mary, why are you like this, that I see your face laughing at one time, but then sad?

And she said to him, It's because I see two people in my eyes. One is crying and mourning, and one is rejoicing and exulting.

3 And they came to the middle of the journey, and Mary said to him, Joseph, take me down from the donkey, because the one who's inside me is pushing to come out.

And he took her down from the donkey and asked her, Where will I take you to give you some privacy? This place is a wilderness.

CHAP. XVIII.

1 *Joseph brings Mary to a cave and seeks a Hebrew midwife.* 2 *He perceives the birds stopping in their flight, the workers at their food not moving, the sheep standing still, the shepherd fixed and immoveable, and young goats with their mouths in the water but not drinking.*

nd he found a cave there, brought her (to it), stationed his sons with her, and went to look for a Hebrew midwife in the region of Bethlehem.

2 Now I, Joseph, was wandering but not wandering. And I looked up to the dome of heaven and saw it standing still, and into the sky, and I was astonished to see that even the birds of heaven were still. And I looked at the ground and saw a bowl lying there, and workers reclining, and their hands were in the bowl, and they were chewing but not chewing, and they were picking up food but not picking up food, and they were bringing it to their mouths but not bringing it to their mouths. Rather, all their faces were looking up.

And I saw sheep being driven, but the sheep stood still. And the shepherd lifted his hand to strike them, but his hand was raised. And I looked into the torrent of the river and saw young goats, and their mouths were in the water but not drinking.

And suddenly, everything resumed its course.

CHAP. XIX.

1 *Joseph finds a midwife.* 2 *A bright cloud overshadows the cave. A great light appears in the cave until the infant is born.* 3 *The midwife goes out and tells Salome that she has seen a virgin give birth. Salome doubts.*

nd look! A woman was coming down from the mountain, and she asked me, Man, where are you going?

And I said, I'm seeking a Hebrew midwife.

And in response she asked me, Are you from Israel?

And I said to her, Yes.

Then she asked, And who's the one giving birth in the cave?

And I said, My fiancé.

And she asked me, She's not your wife?

And I said to her, Mary was nurtured in the Temple of the Lord, and it was decided by lot that she would be my wife, yet she's not my wife; but she's conceived from the Holy Spirit.

And the midwife asked, Really?

And Joseph said to her, Come and see.

And the midwife went with him.

2 And they stood in front of the cave, and a bright cloud overshadowed the cave. And the midwife said, My soul is magnified today, because my eyes have seen something wonderful. Salvation has been born to Israel!

And immediately the cloud withdrew from the cave, and a great light appeared in the cave, so that their eyes couldn't bear it. And a little later, the light withdrew until an infant appeared. And he came and took the breast of his mother, Mary.

And the midwife cried out and said, How great today is for me, that I've seen this new miracle!

3 And the midwife went out from the cave, and Salome met her.

And she said to her, Salome, Salome, I have to describe a new sight to you. A virgin has given birth, which is against her nature!

And Salome said, As the Lord my God lives, unless I examine her condition, I won't believe that the virgin has given birth.

CHAP. XX.

1 *Salome's hand withers* 2 *and she prays to the Lord.* 3 *She's cured,* 4 *but warned not to report what she's seen.*

nd the midwife went in and said, Mary, position yourself, because there's no small test coming concerning you.

And Salome examined her. And Salome cried out and said, Woe because of my lawlessness and my unbelief! Because I've tested the living God, and look! My hand is on fire and falling away from me!

2 And she dropped to her knees before the Lord. She said, God of my ancestors, remember me, that I've descended from Abraham, Isaac, and Jacob. Don't make an example of me to the people of Israel, but give me the back to the poor, because you

know, Lord, that in your name I've healed people, and I've received my wages from you.

3 And look! An angel of the Lord appeared. It said to her, Salome, Salome, the Lord of all has heard your prayer. Bring your hand to the child and lift him up, and you'll receive salvation and joy.

4 And Salome joyfully went to the child and lifted him up. She said, I worship him, because a great king has been born to Israel. And immediately Salome was healed, and she left the cave justified.

And look! A voice was saying, Salome, Salome, don't report the wonderful things you've seen until the child comes into Jerusalem.

CHAP. XXI.

1 *Magi come from the East.* 2 *Herod is alarmed; desires that if they find the child, they report to him.* 3 *They visit the cave and offer the child their treasure, and being warned in a dream, don't return to Herod, but go home another way.*

nd look! Joseph prepared to go out into Judea when a great commotion arose in Bethlehem of Judea. For magi came and said, Where is the king of the Jews? For we saw his star in the East and have come to worship him.

2 And when Herod heard, he was disturbed, and he sent officers to the magi, and sent for the chief priests and questioned them in his palace. He asked them, What has been written about the Christ? Where will he be born?

They said to him, In Bethlehem of Judea, for this is what's written. And he set (the chief priests) free.

And he questioned the magi, saying to them, What sign did you see about the one who's been born king?

And the magi said, We saw an immense star shining among the other stars and dimming them so much that they weren't even visible. And so we knew that a king had been born for Israel, and we came to worship him.

And Herod said to them, Go and search, and if you find him, report to me so that I can also come and worship him.

3 And the magi went, and look! The star they had seen in the East led them until they came to the cave, and it stood over the head of the cave. And when they saw him with his mother Mary, the magi took

gifts from their bags: gold, and frankincense, and myrrh.

And having been warned by the angel not to go into Judea, they returned to their country by another way.

CHAP. XXII.

1 *Herod is angry, orders the infants to be killed.* 2 *Mary puts her infant in a manger for cows.* 3 *Elizabeth flees with her son John to the hills. A mountain miraculously splits and receives them.*

hen Herod saw that he had been tricked by the magi, he was angry. He sent out his killers, telling them to kill all the infants two years old and younger.

2 And when Mary heard that the infants were being killed, she was afraid. She took her child, wrapped him in cloths, and put him in a manger for cows.

3 And when Elizabeth heard that John was sought, she took him up into the hills and looked around for somewhere to hide him, but there wasn't a hiding place. Then Elizabeth groaned and said, Mountain of God, take a mother with her child, because Elizabeth was unable to go up higher. And immediately, the mountain split and took her, and a light shone through the mountain for her. For an angel of the Lord was with them, protecting them.

CHAP. XXIII.

1 *Herod is incensed at the escape of John.* 3 *He causes Zechariah to be murdered in the Temple of the Lord.*

ut Herod asked for John and sent officers to Zechariah. They said to him, Where are you hiding your son?

But in response he said to them, I'm a minister of God, and I sit in God's Temple. How should I know where my son is?

2 And his officers went away and reported all these things to Herod. And Herod was angry, and said, His son is about to be king over Israel!

And he sent his officers again, to say to him, Tell me the truth. Where's your son? You know that your life is in my hand.

And the officers went away and reported these things to him.

3 And Zechariah said, I'm a martyr of God if you shed my blood, because the Lord will receive my spirit, since you'll be spilling innocent blood at the entrance of the Temple of the Lord.

And around daybreak, Zechariah was murdered, and the people of Israel didn't know that he was murdered.

CHAP. XXIV.

1 *The priests wait for Zechariah.* 3 *The panels of the temple cry out, Zechariah's corpse isn't found, and his blood is petrified. Israel mourns for him,* 4 *and Simeon is chosen his successor by lot.*

ut at the hour of greeting, the priests came, and Zechariah didn't meet them to bless them as was customary. And the priests stood around for Zechariah, waiting to greet him with a blessing and to glorify the Most High God.

2 But when he delayed, they were all afraid. But one of them gathered the courage to go into the sanctuary and saw blood clotted beside the altar of the Lord. And a voice was saying, Zechariah has been murdered, and his blood won't be wiped away until his avenger comes!

When he heard this saying, he was afraid, and he went and reported to the priests what he had seen and heard.

3 And they gathered their courage and went and saw what had taken place. And the panels of the Temple cried out, and (the priests) ripped their clothes from top to bottom. And they didn't find his corpse, but they found his blood had turned to stone. And they were afraid, and they went out and reported to all the people that Zechariah had been murdered. And when all the tribes of the people heard, they mourned him and wept three days and three nights.

4 And after three days, the priests held a council about who should replace Zechariah. And the lot fell to Simeon, for he was told by the Holy Spirit that he wouldn't see death until he saw the Christ in the flesh.

CHAP. XXV.

1 *James wrote this history.*

ow I, James, wrote this history in Jerusalem when there was a commotion over Herod's death. I went into the wilderness until the commotion in Jerusalem had died down. I was glorifying the Lord God, who gave me the wisdom to write this history.

2 And grace will be with all who fear the Lord. Amen.

THE INFANCY GOSPEL OF THOMAS

The Infancy Gospel of Thomas was originally written in the second century. Manuscripts of this Gospel currently exist in several languages, dating as early as the fifth century in Syriac. Scholars have divided the Greek manuscripts into four recensions: Greek A, Greek B, Greek D, and Greek S. The earliest Greek manuscript (the Greek S recension) is Hagios Saba 259, dating to the eleventh century.

Most translations are based on Tischendorf's nineteenth-century transcript of the Greek A recension, but this translation is based on the earliest Greek manuscript, Hagios Saba 259. In this manuscript, Chapter X actually appears after Chapter XVI, but has been moved to its current location to track with existing translations. Also, Hagios Saba 259 doesn't include Chapters XVII and XVIII, so in this translation, those two chapters have been translated from the Greek A recension. For more information, see my book *The Infancy Gospels: Exploring Jesus' Family*, published in 2019.

The most shocking stories in this Gospel depict the boy Jesus striking down other children in Chapters III and IV with death curses that aren't reversed until Chapter VIII. Of particular interest is the story of the boy Jesus creating live sparrows out of clay in Chapter II, which is also found in the Qur'an.

CHAP. I.

1 *Prologue by Thomas the Israelite.*

I am Thomas the Israelite. I thought it necessary to make known to all the gentile brothers (and sisters) all the things done by our Lord Jesus Christ in the village of Nazareth, after he was born in our region of Bethlehem. This is the beginning:

CHAP. II.

1 *Jesus miraculously cleans the water* 2 *and plays with*

clay sparrows, which he animates on the Sabbath.

he child Jesus was five years old. After it rained, he was playing at the ford of a flowing stream. And stirring up the dirty waters, he gathered them into pools, and he made them clean and excellent, ordering them by word alone—and not ordering them by a deed.

2 Then, having taken soft clay from the mud, he formed twelve sparrows from it. But it was the Sabbath when he did these things, and many children were with him.

3 But a certain Jew saw the child Jesus with the other children doing these things. He went to Joseph his father and slandered the child Jesus, saying that he made clay on the Sabbath, which isn't permissible, and formed twelve sparrows.

4 And Joseph went and rebuked (Jesus). He said, Why are you doing these things on the Sabbath?

But Jesus clapped his hands, ordering the birds with a shout in front of all, and said, Go, take flight like living beings! And the sparrows, taking flight, went away squawking.

5 And having seen this, the Pharisee was amazed, and he reported it to all his friends.

CHAP. III.

2 *Jesus curses a boy who destroyed his pools.*

nd the son of Annas the high priest asked (Jesus), Why are you doing such a thing on the Sabbath? And having taken a willow twig, he destroyed the pools and drained the water which Jesus had gathered, and he dried up their gatherings.

2 But having seen what had happened, Jesus said to him, Your fruit (will have) no root, and your shoot will be withered like a scorched branch in a violent wind!

3 And immediately that child withered away.

CHAP. IV.

1 *Jesus curses another boy,* 2 *whose parents blame Joseph.*

rom there he was going with his father Joseph, and someone running struck his shoulder. And Jesus said to him, May you be cursed because of your leader!

And immediately he died.

And the people who saw that he had died immediately cried out and asked, From where was this child born, that his word becomes deed?

2 And when the parents of the dead child saw what had happened, they blamed his father Joseph. They said, From wherever you have this child, you can't live with us in this village. If you want to be here, teach him to bless and not to curse, because our child has been taken away from us.

CHAP. V.

1 *Jesus causes blindness to fall on his accusers,* 2 *for which Joseph pulls him by the ear.*

nd Joseph asked Jesus, Why do you say such things, and they suffer and hate us?

And the child said to Joseph, Since you know wise words, you're not ignorant of where they came from; <they were spoken about a five-year-old.> And they won't be raised, and these will receive their punishment.

And immediately those accusing him became blind.

2 And Joseph took (Jesus') ear and pulled hard.

3 And Jesus said to him, It's enough for you seek and find me, and not, beyond that, to scourge me by having taken on a natural ignorance. You haven't clearly seen me, why I'm yours. Look! I've been subdued before you.

CHAP. VI.

2 *Zacchaeus offers to teach Jesus.* 5 *People are amazed by Jesus.* 8 *His teacher strikes him on the head.* 9 *Jesus teaches his teacher.*

teacher named Zacchaeus (was) standing (there), hearing Jesus saying these things to his father Joseph, and he was very amazed.

2 And he said to Joseph, Come, give him (to me), brother, so that he may be taught letters, and so that he may know all knowledge, and learn to love those his own age, and honor old age and respect elders, so that he may acquire a yearning for children, teaching them in return.

3 But Joseph asked the teacher, And who can control this child and teach him? Don't think of him as a small person, brother.

But the teacher said, Give him to me, brother, and don't let him concern you.

4 And the child Jesus looked at them and said to the teacher this speech: Being a teacher comes naturally to you, but you're a stranger to the name with which you're named, because I'm outside of you and I'm within you on account of the nobility of my birth in the flesh. But you, a lawyer, don't know the law.

And he said to Joseph, When you were born, I existed, standing beside you so that as a father you may be taught a teaching by me which no one else knows or can teach. And you'll bear the name of salvation.

5 And the Jews cried out and said to him, Oh new and incredible wonder! The child is perhaps five years old, and oh, what words he says! We've never known such words. No one—neither a lawyer nor a Pharisee—has spoken like this child.

6 In response the child asked them, Why are you amazed? Or rather, why don't you believe the things I've said to you? The truth is that I, who was created before this world, know accurately when you were born, and your fathers, and their fathers.

7 And all the people who heard this were speechless, no longer able to talk to him. But he went up to them, skipped around, and said, I was playing with you because I know you're small-minded, and amazed with small things.

8 Now when they seemed comforted by the child's encouragement, the teacher said to his father, Come, bring him into the school. I'll teach him letters.

And Joseph took his hand and led him into the school. And the teacher flattered him, brought him into the school, and Zacchaeus wrote the alphabet for him and began to teach him, saying the same letter frequently. But the child didn't answer him.

And the teacher became irritated and struck him on the head.

And the child became irritated and said to him, I want to teach you rather than be taught by you, since I know the letters you're teaching more accurately. To me these things are like a noisy gong or a clanging cymbal that doesn't bring out the sound, nor the glory, nor the power of understanding.

9 When the child's anger ceased, he said all the letters by himself, from the alpha to

the omega, very skillfully. And looking straight at the teacher he asked, If you don't know the nature of the alpha, how can you teach another the beta? Hypocrite! If you know, first teach me the alpha, and then I will trust you to speak of the beta. Then he began to teach the teacher about the first element. And he couldn't say anything to him.

10 While many listened, he said to the teacher, Listen, Teacher, and understand the arrangement of the first element. Now, notice how it has sharp lines and a middle stroke, which you see pointing, standing with legs apart, coming together, going out, dragging behind, lifting up, dancing around, <…>, in triple rhythm, two-cornered, of the same form, of the same thickness, of the same family, raised, balanced, isometric, of equal proportions. These are the lines of the alpha.

CHAP. VII.

1 *Jesus' teacher laments,* 4 *confesses that Jesus is great.*

hen the teacher heard such good familiarity (and) such lines of the first letter Jesus talked about, he was baffled by such teaching and his defense. And the teacher said, Woe is me! Woe is me! I've been baffled and am miserable. I've brought shame on myself, taking on this child.

2 Take (him) away from me, brother, because I can't bear his gaze, nor the clarity of his word. This child is simply not of this earth. He can even tame fire! Perhaps this child existed before the creation of the world. What kind of womb bore him? What kind of mother raised him? I don't know. Woe is me, brother! He stupefies me. My mind can't follow him. I've deceived myself, thrice-unhappy as I am. I thought to gain a disciple, and I'm found having a teacher.

3 Friends, I ponder my shame, old man that I am, that I've been defeated by a child. I should be cast out and die, or flee this village because of this child. I can't be seen any longer among everyone, especially those who saw that I was defeated by a very small child. But what can I say or tell anyone about the lines of the first element? The truth is that I don't know, friends, because I understand neither the beginning nor the end!

4 Therefore, brother Joseph, lead him away with sal-

vation into your house, because this child is a great thing—whether a god or an angel or whatever else I might say—I don't know.

CHAP. VIII.

2 *Jesus saves all who had fallen under his curse.*

he child Jesus laughed and said, Now may the barren bear fruit, the blind see, and the foolish in heart find understanding: that I'm here from above, so that I may deliver those below and call them up, just as the one who sent me to you has ordered me.

2 And immediately all who had fallen under his curse were saved. And no one dared to provoke him from then on.

CHAP. IX.

1 *Zeno falls and dies.* 3 *Jesus temporarily raises him to prove he didn't push him down.*

nd again, after many days, Jesus was playing with other children on a certain roof of an upstairs room. But one of the children fell and died. And the other children saw this and went into their houses. And they left Jesus alone.

2 And the parents of the child who had died came and accused Jesus. They said, You pushed down our child!

But Jesus said, I didn't push him down.

3 And they were raging and shouting. Jesus came down from the roof and stood beside the body and cried out in a loud voice: Zeno, Zeno (because this was his name), rise and say whether I pushed you down.

And he rose and said, No, sir.

And they saw and were amazed.

And again, Jesus said to him, Fall asleep!

And the parents of the child praised God and worshipped the child Jesus.

CHAP. X.

1 *A woodcutter dies and* 2 *Jesus heals him.*

gain, a certain young man was splitting wood into equal parts. And he split the bottom of his foot, bled out, and died.

2 A commotion arose, and Jesus ran there. Forcing his way through the crowd, he

seized the stricken foot, and immediately it was healed. And he said to the young man, Go, split your wood.

3 And the crowds saw and were amazed and said, For he saved many souls from death, and he will continue to save all the days of his life.

CHAP. XI.

2 *Jesus carries water in his cloak.*

nd the child Jesus was about seven years old, and his mother Mary sent him to fill up water. But there was a great crowd at the water cistern, and the pitcher was struck and broke.

2 But Jesus spread out the cloak he was wearing, filled it with water, and carried it to his mother. And Mary saw what sign Jesus had done. She kissed him and said, Lord, my God, bless our child, because they were afraid that someone might bewitch him.

CHAP. XII.

2 *Miracle of the harvest.*

nd at the time of the sowing, Joseph sowed seeds, and the child Jesus sowed one measure of wheat.

2 And his father reaped a hundred great measures. And he gave graciously to the poor and the orphans. But Joseph took from Jesus' seeds.

CHAP. XIII.

1 *Joseph works on a bed.* 2 *Jesus miraculously stretches one of the boards.*

ow (Jesus) was about eight years old. And his father, being a carpenter who made ploughs and yokes, took a bed from a certain rich man so that he might make it very great and suitable. And one of the beams, called the <...>, was shorter; it didn't have the (right) length. Joseph was grieved, and didn't know what to do.

The child came to his father and said, Set down the two boards and line them up on your end.

2 And Joseph did just as he told him. And the child Jesus stood at the other end and seized the short board and stretched it. And he made it equal with the other board.

And he said to his father, Don't grieve, but make whatever you want to.

And Joseph embraced and kissed him. He said, Blessed am I, that God gave this child to me.

CHAP. XIV.

1 *Joseph brings Jesus to a second teacher.* 2 *The teacher strikes Jesus, who curses him.*

nd Joseph saw his wisdom and understanding. He didn't want him to be unacquainted with letters, but gave him over to another teacher. And the teacher wrote the alphabet for (Jesus) and said, Say alpha.

2 And the child said, First you tell me what the beta is, and I'll tell you what the alpha is. And the teacher became irritated and struck him. And Jesus cursed him, and the teacher fell and died.

3 And the child went into his house to his parents, and Joseph called (Jesus') mother and ordered her not to set (Jesus) free from the house so that those who provoke him may not die.

CHAP. XV.

1 *A third teacher offers to teach Jesus.* 2 *Jesus impresses with his teaching.* 4 *Jesus saves his previous teacher.*

nd after some days, again another teacher said to (Jesus') father Joseph: Come, brother, give him to me in the school so that with flattery I can teach him letters.

And Joseph said to him, If you have courage, brother, take him with salvation.

And the teacher took the child by the hand and led him away with much fear and concern. And the child went gladly.

2 And entering the school, (Jesus) found a book lying on the lectern. And he took it, but he didn't read what was written in it, because it wasn't from God's Law. But he opened his mouth and uttered words so impressive that the teacher seated opposite heard him very gladly and encouraged him so that he might say more. And the crowd standing there was amazed at his holy words.

3 And Joseph ran quickly to the school, suspecting that this teacher was no longer inexperienced and suffered. But the teacher said to Joseph, So that you know, brother, I indeed took your child as a disciple, but he's full of much

grace and wisdom. So, brother, lead him away with salvation into your house.

4 And (Jesus) said to the teacher, Since you spoke correctly and testified correctly, the one struck down will also be saved because of you. And immediately that teacher also was saved. And taking the child, (Joseph) led (Jesus) away into his house.

CHAP. XVI.

2 *Jesus heals James' snakebite.*

nd James went into the grove to tie up sticks so that they might make bread. And Jesus went with him. And as they were gathering the sticks, a terrible snake bit James on his hand.

2 And he was sprawled out and dying. And the child Jesus ran to James and blew on the bite, and immediately the bite was healed. And the beast was destroyed, and James was saved.

CHAP. XVII.

1 *A baby dies, and Jesus raises him.*

nd after these things, in Joseph's neighborhood a certain baby was sick and died. And his mother wept very much.

But Jesus heard that there was great grief and commotion, and he ran quickly. And he found the child dead, touched his chest, and said, I say to you, baby, don't die, but live, and be with your mother.

And (the baby) looked up immediately and laughed. And (Jesus) said to the mother, Take your child, give him milk, and remember me.

2 And the crowd standing there was amazed, and said, The truth is, this child is a god or an angel, because his every word becomes a deed!

And Jesus went away again and played with the children.

CHAP. XVIII.

1 *Jesus raises a builder from the dead.*

nd after some time, a building was being constructed. There was a great commotion, and Jesus got up and went there.

And seeing a man lying dead, (Jesus) seized (the man's) hand and said, I tell you, man, rise and do your

Albrecht Altdorfer, Christ Disputing with the Doctors
ca. 1513, National Gallery of Art

work. And (the man) immediately rose and worshipped him.

2 And the crowd saw and was amazed. They said, This child is from heaven, for he saved many souls from death, and he will continue to save all the days of his life.

CHAP. XIX.

1 *Jesus' parents take him to Jerusalem for the Passover.* 2 *They find him in the Temple.* 5 *Jesus is obedient to his parents.*

nd when Jesus was twelve years old, his parents went, according to custom, to Jerusalem for the festival of the Passover. But during their return, Jesus stayed behind in Jerusalem. And his parents didn't know.

2 And assuming him to be in the traveling company, they went a day's journey and searched for him among their known relatives. And not finding him, they returned to Jerusalem and searched for him.

And after three days, they found him in the Temple sitting in the middle of the teachers, and listening to them and questioning them. And those hearing him were surprised how he questioned the elders and explained the main points of the Law and the riddles and the parables of the prophets.

3 And his mother asked him, Child, what have you done to us? Look, we've been searching for you in pain and grieving.

And Jesus asked, Why were you looking for me? Didn't you know that it's necessary for me to be in the place of my Father?

4 And the scribes and the Pharisees asked Mary, You're the mother of this child?

She said, I am.

And they said to her, Blessed are you that the Lord God has blessed the fruit of your womb, because we've never seen such wisdom of praise and glory of virtue.

5 And Jesus stood up and followed his mother from there, and was obedient to his parents. And she treasured all these things, pondering them in her heart.

And Jesus advanced in wisdom and maturity and grace before God and humans. To whom be the [glory …]

Appendix: Gnostic Gospels?

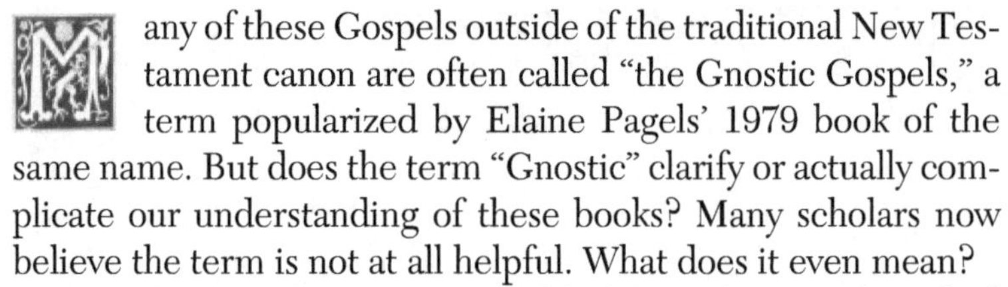

Many of these Gospels outside of the traditional New Testament canon are often called "the Gnostic Gospels," a term popularized by Elaine Pagels' 1979 book of the same name. But does the term "Gnostic" clarify or actually complicate our understanding of these books? Many scholars now believe the term is not at all helpful. What does it even mean?

People use "Gnosticism" as a label for a "heresy" described by ancient "heresy hunters" (heresiologists) of the church, including Irenaeus of Lyons, Hippolytus of Rome, Tertullian of Carthage, and Epiphanius of Salamis. Until the middle of the twentieth century, these "church fathers" remained the primary historical sources for this apparently loose collection of movements. The relatively recent term "Gnosticism" comes from the ancient label "Gnostic," from the Greek word *gnōsis*, which means "knowledge." Irenaeus had based his work on 1 Timothy 6:20, which warns against "the empty chatter and opposing ideas of so-called knowledge (*gnōseōs*)." But although Irenaeus describes something "called Gnostic," many scholars today question whether there ever was a specific movement or group of movements that could be summed up under the rubric of "Gnosticism."

Until recently, scholars building on the work of these "church fathers" tried to define ancient "Gnosticism" by summarizing key ideas stemming from a dualistic view of spirit and matter—spirit being inherently good and matter being inherently evil. If God is spiritual (good), then who could have created a physical universe (evil)? Apparently, a "demiurge" or "craftsman," a divine being lower than the true God. This "demiurge," which was ignorant (at best) or evil (at worst), would then have enslaved good spirits in the prison of human bodies. How, then, could these good spirits escape their evil physical bodies and ascend to heaven? By receiving the teaching of the spiritual Christ, who could not have been truly human and so could not have died on the cross or risen from the dead, as traditional Christianity has maintained. The practical ramifications of these teachings, it was thought, led to one of two extremes: either an "ascetic" ethic that all material pleasure is also evil, or a "libertine" ethic that since matter is evil anyway, whatever spiritual people do in the flesh is irrelevant.

However, the discovery of the Nag Hammadi Library in Egypt in 1945 has expanded our available source material for the various movements previously lumped together under the label of "Gnosticism." Scholars now have direct access to many of the texts these so-called "Gnostics" wrote and used. At first, scholars read these texts through the lens of their contemporary critics. But more recently, some have questioned these traditional interpretations. They point out that the Nag Hammadi texts don't all represent the same viewpoint, and furthermore that none of them individually contains all the ideas described above. Several don't even contain any of these views. In short, many question whether something called "Gnosticism" ever existed outside the creative imaginations of heresy hunters and church historians.

For Further Reading

FOR FURTHER READING

Aasgaard, Reidar, *The Childhood of Jesus: Decoding the Apocryphal Infancy Gospel of Thomas* (James Clarke & Co., 2010)

Barnstone, Willis, *The Restored New Testament: A New Translation with Commentary, Including the Gnostic Gospels Thomas, Mary, and Judas* (W.W. Norton & Company, 2009)

Bernhard, Andrew E., *Other Early Christian Gospels: A Critical Edition of the Surviving Greek Manuscripts* (T&T Clark International, 2007)

Borg, Marcus, *The Lost Gospel Q: The Original Sayings of Jesus* (Ulysses Press, 1996)

Bourgeault, Cynthia, *The Wisdom Jesus: Transforming Heart and Mind—A New Perspective on Christ and His Message* (Shambhala, 2008)

Brannan, Rick, *Greek Apocryphal Gospels, Fragments, and Agrapha: Texts and Transcriptions* (Lexham Press, 2013)

Burke, Tony, *De Infantia Iesu Evangelium Thomae Graece* (Brepols, 2010)

Cameron, Ron, *Sayings Traditions in the Apocryphon of James* (Fortress Press, 1984)

Davies, Stevan, *The Gospel of Thomas and Christian Wisdom: Second Edition* (Bardic Press, 2005)

Davies, Stevan, *The Gospel of Thomas Annotated & Explained* (Skylight Paths, 2002)

De Boer, Esther, *Mary Magdalene: Beyond the Myth* (Trinity Press International, 1997)

DeConick, April D., *The Thirteenth Apostle: What the Gospel of Judas Really Says* (Continuum, 2007, rev. ed. 2009)

De Strycker, Éimile, *La Forme la plus ancienne du Protévangile de Jacques* (Société des Bollandistes, 1961)

Ehrman, Bart D., *The Lost Gospel of Judas Iscariot: A New Look at Betrayer and Betrayed* (Oxford University Press), 2006

Ehrman, Bart D. and Zlatko Pleše, *The Apocryphal Gospels: Texts and Translations* (Oxford University Press, 2011)

Foster, Paul, *The Gospel of Peter: Introduction, Critical Edition and Commentary* (Brill, 2010)

Frilingos, Christopher A., *Jesus, Mary, and Joseph: Family Trouble in the Infancy Gospels* (University of Pennsylvania Press, 2017)

Funk, Robert W., Roy W. Hoover, and the Jesus Seminar, *The Five Gospels: The Search for the Authentic Words of Jesus* (Harper-SanFrancisco, 1993)

Gathercole, Simon, *The Apocryphal Gospels* (Penguin Books, 2021)

Grobel, Kendrick, *The Gospel of Truth: A Valentinian Meditation on the Gospel* (Abingdon Press, 1960)

Hock, Ronald F., *The Infancy Gospels of James and Thomas* (Pole-bridge Press), 1995

Jenott, Lance, "The Book of the Foreigner from Codex Tchacos," *Bulletin of the American Society of Papyrologists* 57 (2020), 235-276

Jenott, Lance, *The Gospel of Judas: Coptic Text, Translation, and Historical Interpretation of the 'Betrayer's Gospel'* (Mohr Siebeck, 2011)

Kasser, Rodolphe, and Gregor Wurst, *The Gospel of Judas, Critical Edition: Together with the Letter of Peter to Philip, James, and a Book of Allogenes from Codex Tchacos* (National Geographic, 2007)

King, Karen L., *The Gospel of Mary of Magdala: Jesus and the First Woman Apostle* (Polebridge Press, 2003)

King, Karen L., *What Is Gnosticism?* (Belknap, 2003)

Krosney, Herbert, Marvin Meyer, and Gregor Wurst, "Preliminary Report on New Fragments of Codex Tchacos," *Early Christianity* 1 (2010), 282-294

Layton, Bentley, *The Gnostic Scriptures* (Doubleday, 1987)

Leloup, Jean-Yves, *The Gospel of Mary Magdalene* (Inner Traditions, 2002)

Leloup, Jean-Yves, *The Gospel of Philip: Jesus, Mary Magdalene, and the Gnosis of Sacred Union* (Inner Traditions, 2004)

Leloup, Jean-Yves, *The Gospel of Thomas: The Gnostic Wisdom of Jesus* (Inner Traditions, 2004)

Lundhaug, Hugo, *Images of Rebirth: Cognitive Poetics and Transformational Soteriology in the Gospel of Philip and the Exegesis of the Soul* (Brill, 2010)

Magnusson, Jörgen, *Rethinking the Gospel of Truth: A Study of Its Eastern Valentinian Setting* (Uppsala University, 2006)

Meyer, Marvin, *The Gospel of Thomas: The Hidden Sayings of Jesus* (HarperSanFrancisco, 1992)

Meyer, Marvin, with Esther A. de Boer, *The Gospels of Mary: The Secret Tradition of Mary Magdalene, the Companion of Jesus* (HarperSanFrancisco, 2004)

Meyer, Marvin, ed., *The Nag Hammadi Scriptures* (HarperOne, 2007)

Miller, Robert J., ed., *The Complete Gospels: Fourth Edition* (Polebridge Press, 2010)

Pagels, Elaine, *Beyond Belief: The Secret Gospel of Thomas* (Vintage Books, 2004)

Pagels, Elaine, *The Gnostic Gospels* (Random House, 1979)

Pagels, Elaine and Karen L. King, *Reading Judas: The Gospel of Judas and the Shaping of Christianity* (Viking, 2007)

Patterson, Stephen J., *The Gospel of Thomas and Jesus* (Polebridge Press, 1993)

Robinson, James M., ed., *The Nag Hammadi Library in English,* 4th rev. ed. (Brill, 1996)

Robinson, James M., Paul Hoffman, and John S., Kloppenborg, eds., *The Critical Edition of Q: Synopsis including the Gospels of Matthew and Luke, Mark and Thomas with English, German, and French Translations of Q and Thomas* (Peeters, 2000)

Schneemelcher, Wilhelm, ed., *New Testament Apocrypha Volume One: Gospels and Related Writings, Revised Edition* (Westminster John Knox Press, 1991 [2003])

Smith, Andrew Philip, *The Gospel of Philip: Annotated & Explained* (Skylight Paths, 2005)

Taussig, Hal, ed., *A New New Testament* (Houghton Mifflin Harcourt, 2013)

Valantasis, Richard, *The Gospel of Thomas* (Routledge, 1997)

Vanden Eykel, Eric M., *"But Their Faces Were All Looking Up": Author and Reader in the Protevangelium of James* (T&T Clark, 2016)

Williams, Michael Allen, *Rethinking "Gnosticism": An Argument for Dismantling a Dubious Category* (Princeton University Press, 1996)

Wurst, Gregor, "Weitere neue Fragmente aus Codex Tchacos: Zum 'Buch des Allogenes' und zu Corpus Hermeticum XIII," in E. E. Popkes and G. Wurst, eds., *Judasevangelium und Codex Tchacos: Studien zur religionsgeschichtlichen Verortung* (Mohr Siebeck, 2012), 1-12

Zinner, Samuel, *The Gospel of Thomas in the Light of Early Jewish, Christian, and Islamic Esoteric Trajectories: with a contextualized commentary and a new translation of the Thomas Gospel* (The Matheson Trust, 2011)

Made in United States
Troutdale, OR
08/21/2024